TOUCHING HEAVEN

TOUCHING HEAVEN

By Lee Roberson

**Pastor Emeritus of the
Highland Park Baptist Church,
Chattanooga, Tennessee**

**Chancellor of
Tennessee Temple University**

SWORD of the LORD
PUBLISHERS

P. O. Box 1099, Murfreesboro, TN 37133

Printed and Bound in the United States of America

Table of Contents

Preface

Our beloved Brother Lester Roloff once said,

"PRAYER IS INSTANT CONTACT WITH HEAVEN."

Jesus, in giving instruction on prayer and in the example prayer, said we pray to "Our Father which art in HEAVEN."

"After this manner therefore pray ye: Our Father which art in heaven, Hallowed be thy name."—Matt. 6:9.

"These words spake Jesus, and lifted up his eyes to heaven, and said, Father, the hour is come; glorify thy Son, that thy Son also may glorify thee."—John 17:1.

"Every time you pray, you touch Heaven."

Read it again; "Every time you pray, you touch Heaven."

Some "praying" is just the saying of words, perhaps impressive and beautiful, but just words—but true prayer touches Heaven!

When you touch Heaven:
Peace comes to your heart.
New power is yours.
A new solution to the most serious problem is yours.
Loneliness is gone.
Fear is dispelled.
A new vision is given.
A new determination to glorify God is imparted to you.

Prayer is touching Heaven! *"Our Father which art in heaven. . . . "*

—Dr. Lee Roberson

Introduction

This volume is totally given to the subject of prayer. In it you will find sermons on Bible passages dealing with prayer, how to pray, prayer promises, exhortations to pray and illustrations of God's mighty working in answer to prayer.

Dr. John R. Rice said, "All our failures are prayer failures." Perhaps none of us who name the name of Christ really grasp the potential that is ours because of the access we have to the throne of our great God through the Lord Jesus Christ.

These sermons were preached and this book is written in the hope that it will bless, inform and challenge those who know Jesus Christ as Saviour to exercise more fully the privilege that has been given them and the power available through prayer. In these pages Dr. Roberson speaks humbly, yet confidently, not only on the basis of Bible truth, but also from personal experience, about the importance of prayer and the dramatic results that come in answer to prayer.

The last fifty pages of this book are a reprint of a booklet compiled by Dr. Roberson of illustrations, quotes, poems and sayings about prayer.

Sword of the Lord Publishers is thrilled and honored to have the opportunity of working with Dr. Roberson in making this volume available to Christian readers everywhere. We join him in asking God to use it mightily for His own glory in the lives of His people.

Dr. John Reynolds
Assistant Editor
Sword of the Lord

"O Lord, by whom we come to God,
The Life, the Truth, the Way,
The path of PRAYER Thyself hast trod;
Lord, teach us now to pray."

The Heart of Every Prayer

"Thy kingdom come. Thy will be done in earth, as it is in heaven."—Matt. 6:10.

"And he went a little farther, and fell on his face, and prayed, saying, O my Father, if it be possible, let this cup pass from me: nevertheless not as I will, but as thou wilt."—Matt. 26:39.

The Christian must learn to walk after Jesus in all things: in purity of heart, in singleness of purpose, in animosity toward sin, in submission to the Father's will. Yes, and especially in prayer.

Our Saviour taught us in the model prayer, 'Pray thus, "Thy will be done in earth as it is in heaven." '

Our Saviour gave us an example in praying in the garden of Gethsemane: "Not as I will, but as thou wilt."

What is the heart of every prayer? "Not as I will, but as thou wilt." That prayer must come from the depth of the heart. It cannot be offered in a shallow or hypocritical way. It means nothing unless it comes from the depth of the soul.

This prayer may be offered in empty repetition, that is, it may be said many times but without any meaning. Quite often when we hear Christians pray, "Father, Thy will be done," they neither think what they are saying nor calculate the full meaning of such a prayer.

At times this prayer might be offered with a halfhearted emphasis. We want God's will to be done, but certain things we want for ourselves. Beware of praying in a shallow or halfhearted fashion.

This prayer must be offered with soul-searching earnestness.

First, we must consider our own hearts and determine that God shall have first place. Second, we should give consideration to the cost of praying, "Thy will be done."

Actually, all prayer is as nothing, less than foolishness, unless we want God's will to be done. The desire for self-gain or worldly aggrandizement will often keep us from praying as God would have us pray.

Now, let us see just a few things this prayer will do.

I. THIS PRAYER STRIKES AT SIN

No one can pray, "Thy will be done," and favor sin. This prayer will condemn your sin. It will do still more—reveal your sin if you pray in earnestness.

1. *This prayer will show us sin's delusiveness.* How sly and subtle is sin! How insidious does Satan work and lead us into the pathways of sin!

Quite often some person will come to my office and say, "I feel God wants me to do thus and so." When I point out the foolishness of such an action, at once that one will say, "I can see now that I was wrong." Or it may be that he will go away but return and say, "I was wrong about this. I want to go God's way. I made a mistake in my first thought about God's will."

Yes, sin is delusive. So exercise unusual care in dealing with sin.

2. *This prayer will reveal sin's destructiveness.* Nothing is more destructive than sin. Bob Shuler, Methodist preacher of California, clipped a number of items from a daily newspaper and in one week he had the following:

• One mother cut the throat of her eight-month-old baby with a butcher knife. She said the child cried eternally. She told the judge that she smoked a whole pack of cigarettes to quiet her nerves.

• A man killed two women in a parking lot and crowded their bodies into the back of his car. He didn't know why he had done it. "Something possessed me," he said.

• A father threw his three-year-old child from a seven-story window, then calmly went down and drank three beers. When the police picked him up, he was blubbering pitifully about some overpowering desire within him to kill.

• A fiend in army uniform killed and ravished a child in a hotel room while the mother played the slot machines in a tavern on the ground floor. The mother said the last time she saw her child, she was playing near the bar.

• A six-year-old boy beat his baby sister to death with a poker. He said he was tired of hearing her cry all the time while their mother was at the dance.

• A twelve-year-old boy took a revolver from the dresser drawer, shot dead his nine-year-old playmate, took a sleeping pill belonging to his mother, then went to bed. He told the officers, "I never did like the kid."

• A father killed two little girls. He said he had too many, and these two were the puniest.

We all have seen items just as tragic in the papers of our own cities. Week after week the awful destructiveness of sin and the black inroads of its path are well known to us.

3. *This prayer will make us see Satan's delight.* What is the delight of Satan? To damn the souls of men. He works in various ways to bring to pass his own desire to drive men into Hell. He uses the loose living of professing Christians, plus the sins of the world.

A tramp entered a revival service. At the close, when an opportunity was given for testimonies, he arose and said something like this:

> I used to attend this church when I was a boy. My father was an officer here. There were seven of us boys in a Sunday school class, and we liked our teacher. She would take us to her house on Sunday afternoons, and we would have music and refreshments.
>
> She would then amuse us by teaching us to play cards and training us in other worldly amusements. Then we began to gamble and left Sunday school altogether. Two of those boys have been hanged. Three others are in prison. The sixth and I would be in jail if the authorities could get us.

Satan is constantly working to damn the souls of others; and to do so he blinds the eyes of professing Christians so they will fail to see the error of their ways.

But now note this: I care not who you are, what may be your background or your type of training, if you pray, "Thy will be done," you will be against sin. You will hate your own wrongdoing and the wrongdoing of others. You will seek to be free from sin and to lead others to the same freedom.

II. THIS PRAYER STIRS THE LAZY AND THE INDIFFERENT

There is no sin so prevalent in this day as the sin of indifference. Worldliness is rank, but indifference touches the masses.

Indifference can never be the will of God. Many Christians are indifferent! Face your condition. This is not the will of God for you.

Perhaps we should consider for a moment why people are indifferent.

1. *Indifference comes out of small vision of Christ.* Machine-made religions can never reveal Christ to the people. Heavy denominational programs cannot reveal the Saviour. Christians become indifferent when they fail to see the greatness of the Son of God.

Years ago I used to try to quote a poem which contained these words:

> **When Jesus came to Chattanooga,**
>   **They simply passed Him by;**
> **Then never hurt a hair of Him,**
>   **They only let Him die.**
> **For men had grown more tender,**
>   **And they wouldn't give Him pain,**
> **They only passed on down the street**
>   **And left Him in the rain.**

Indifference of this day isn't violent or abusive, but it simply passes Jesus by.

2. *Indifference comes out of poor vision of the lost multitudes.* I care not who you are, if you will let God take over and reveal to you the masses of humanity lost in sin and bound for Hell, your life will change. You cannot be indifferent, nor careless about church attendance, Bible reading or soul winning when you see thousands dying

daily without Christ and dropping into the pit of Hell.

What is God's will for your life? It is that you endeavor to bring others to Him through your faithfulness and your diligent testimony.

3. *Indifference comes from a limited conception of what God expects of you.* Anything less than your best is displeasing to Him. He wants your best in soul winning. He wants your best in consecrated living. He wants the best of all you have.

> **The best we have, is that too much**
> **For Him who gave up all?**
> **The best we are, is it too good**
> **To use at the Master's call?**

Can you pray, "Father, Thy will be done," and really mean it? Don't simply say it, but let it come from your heart. It will cause you to see your own shameful failures and disgraceful lacks and point out how you are doing nothing for Him.

Again, I say, this prayer stirs the lazy and the indifferent.

III. THIS IS THE PRAYER THAT SENDS CHRISTIANS TO THE ENDS OF THE EARTH

1. *This prayer makes missionaries.* God doesn't want everyone to be on a foreign mission field, but He does want some to be there. And if God calls, He expects your ready response. The most miserable person in this world is the one outside the will of God.

Whatever the Heavenly Father desires of you, give your glad obedience. If He wants you to go to the ends of the earth, then go.

2. *This prayer makes men as fools for Christ's sake.* When Paul said, "We are fools for Christ's sake," he was simply illustrating what this world thinks of one who gives his all to Christ. The rank and file think you are crazy, think you are off the beam and not right mentally.

What a fool was Paul! But wait! He was a fool for Christ's sake. Look at his word in I Corinthians 4:9-16. Study these statements he made. Pray this humble prayer: "O God, let Thy will be done in me. Even though I may seem as a fool, let me be a fool for Christ's sake."

3. *This prayer gives every Christian a concern for the souls of others.*
No man can pray, "Thy will be done," and be unconcerned for the
lost. To pray this prayer will put you in the same category with
Christ, with the Apostles Paul and Peter—Christ who wept over
Jerusalem, Paul who cried over the Jewish people and said, "I have
great heaviness and continual sorrow in my heart"; Peter who
yearned to see others saved and was not ashamed of his suffering,
Peter who said, "Yet if any man suffer as a Christian, let him not
be ashamed, but let him glorify God on this behalf" (I Pet. 4:16).

Let me summarize: "Thy will be done" is the prayer that strikes
at sin, the prayer that stirs the lazy and the indifferent, the prayer
that sends Christians to the ends of the earth. Much more could be
said, but this should cause us to see that here is the heart of every
Christian's prayer. If we cannot pray this, then we are not praying
at all.

In a book written some years ago, I came across this magnifi-
cent story. It told of Paul Bell, whose field of labor was among the
Mexicans in Texas. One Saturday afternoon, taking with him a Mex-
ican deacon of his Mexican Baptist church, he mingled among the
Mexican woodcutters and mine workers who came to Bastrop on
Saturday afternoons.

Coming in contact with a Mexican man in his sixties, Brother
Bell and his deacon engaged him in conversation and found him a
ready listener to the sweetest story ever told. This man was happily
converted. After his conversion he declared, "Since I can neither read
nor write, I want you to help me memorize John 3:16 that you have
used to win me to Jesus. And since our people love to sing, I would
also appreciate your teaching me a gospel song."

With painstaking care, Brother Bell taught this man John 3:16
and the first verse of "What a Friend We Have in Jesus."

In teaching this man about Jesus, Brother Bell, like Philip of
old, carefully instructed the new convert concerning baptism, the
duty of one who had been saved, and what baptism taught. The old
man promised to come to the church, make his public profession and
be baptized.

Three weeks went by, and he did not appear. Brother Bell

wondered just what the reason might be for the delay. In the midst of the morning preaching service on the fourth Sunday, this man walked in, accompanied by five other Mexicans. He didn't stop to be seated but walked down the aisle with his companions and said, "We are all here to be baptized."

In such a brief time he had brought five trophies of the grace of God as the first fruits of his Christian life.

The old man lived for some two years following his conversion. Again and again, when he would come in from his work in the woods, he would bring men with him whom he had won to Christ.

One day Brother Bell was called to his front door. A man said, "There is an old Mexican woodcutter in the woods near Rosanky at the point of death, and he is calling for you."

When Brother Bell arrived at the woodcutter's dwelling, he found his friend near death but fully conscious. The old man's face lighted up at the sight of the preacher. He whispered, "I am so glad to see you. Will you quote my Scripture for me?" As Brother Bell began quoting from John 3:16, the lips of the Mexican followed. When that was finished, the old man said, "Please sing my song for me, also."

Lifting up his voice in song, the preacher began singing in Spanish,

> What a Friend we have in Jesus,
>   All our sins and griefs to bear!
> What a privilege to carry
>   Everything to God in prayer!
> O what peace we often forfeit,
>   O what needless pain we bear,
> All because we do not carry
>   Everything to God in prayer.

As he sang, he noticed the lips of the old Mexican moving; then gradually they ceased. At the end of the verse he turned to find the soul of the aged Christian had slipped away on the wings of the song. But in two short years this illiterate old Mexican had won fifty souls to Christ with one verse of Scripture, one verse of the song, and a great knowledge of Jesus Christ.

My friend, our Saviour wants you, too, to be concerned for others;

and if you pray, "Father, Thy will be done," then surely your heart will be moved to go after others and tell them about Jesus.

Don't Cry Alone

"Casting all your care upon him; for he careth for you."—I Pet. 5:7.

"Cast thy burden upon the Lord, and he shall sustain thee: he shall never suffer the righteous to be moved."—Ps. 55:22.

I read the story of a twenty-nine-year-old bachelor in California who committed suicide. He left a note bearing this message: "*You have to have love to live.*"

The note revealed a lonely, discouraged man who had missed the love of God. He had failed to appropriate the great message found in Jeremiah 31:3, "...Yea, I have loved thee with an everlasting love: therefore with lovingkindness have I drawn thee."

You have missed much of the message of our God if you miss the consciousness of His love for you! Someone said, "God's love is like a stream that never freezes, a fountain that never runs dry, and a sun that never sets."

Awaken your heart to the love of God. "God is love."

David had troubles and heartaches—yes, David cried. The king of Israel—one of God's favorite men—but he cried.

Absalom turned against his father David. Absalom died a strange and violent death. When the message came to David, the king went up into the chamber over the gate and wept. He cried, "O my son Absalom, my son, my son Absalom! would God I had died for thee, O Absalom, my son, my son!" (II Sam. 18:33).

But David did not cry alone! God was there!

Jeremiah, the weeping prophet, the prophet of tears, cried, but not alone. Jeremiah is a book of sobs and tears, a book written by a heartbroken man; but God was with him.

Read Lamentations 1:18; 1:20; 3:26; 5:1. Tears were shed, but he did not cry alone. He felt the presence of God.

Need I mention the greatest name of all—Jesus! "Jesus wept" (John 11:35).

Look at the scene in the Garden of Gethsemane. Christ is praying. He prayed to the Father. He was not alone.

There are some things I know:

I know that life is God-given.

I know that life is precious. It is such a brief life. But remember, this life is just the introduction to eternity.

I know that life is lonely without Christ! All the money, all the fame and power, all of the honors of this world cannot take the place of Christ.

That is exactly what the Holy Spirit brings to us in I Peter 5:6-10.

1. *Our Helper—God:* "Humble yourselves therefore under the mighty hand of God, that he may exalt you in due time: Casting all your care upon him; for he careth for you" (vss. 6, 7).

2. *Our Adversary—Satan:* "Be sober, be vigilant; because your adversary the devil, as a roaring lion, walketh about, seeking whom he may devour: Whom resist stedfast in the faith, knowing that the same afflictions are accomplished in your brethren that are in the world" (vss. 8, 9).

Here is the archenemy of our souls. The Devil is nobody's friend. He is the deceiver of mankind. He fights all men. He hates the Christian and tries to pull him down.

"Submit yourselves therefore to God. Resist the devil, and he will flee from you" (James 4:7).

3. *Our Goal:* "But the God of all grace, who hath called us unto his eternal glory by Christ Jesus, after that ye have suffered a while, make you perfect, stablish, strengthen, settle you" (vs. 10).

Our text is I Peter 5:7. Don't cry alone! From this, there are three practical suggestions:

I. DON'T TRY TO LIVE A SINGLE DAY
WITHOUT THE BIBLE

1. *In the Bible we find the true way of life:* "I am the way...."
"He that believeth on the Son...." From Genesis to Revelation,
Christ is the Life.

2. *The Bible tells us how to live the victorious life.* We need to die
to self and be filled with the Spirit—I must have it; you must have it.

While reading this morning the stories of many successful
preachers, I saw that they had to know the secret of victory.

3. *The Bible tells us how to cleanse our thought-life and our speech:*
Psalm 19:14: "Let the words of my mouth, and the meditation of my
heart, be acceptable in thy sight, O Lord, my strength, and my
redeemer."

This was a battle of mine for years. I wrote Psalm 19:14 on a
piece of paper and put it in my pocket. I quoted it over and over.

4. *The Bible tells us how to have peace of heart.* Jesus said, "My
peace I give unto thee."

Submission! "Thy will be done."

Reading the Bible is a healing balm for the soul.

E. Schuyler English tells of visiting a home in Florida where he
saw an old Bible dated 1877. The name inscribed in the front cover
and the many underlined verses in both Old and New Testaments
revealed that it once belonged to a woman who had undoubtedly been
a devout Christian.

Tucked within its pages were some slips of paper that supplied
additional information about her life. One indicated that in 1883 she
had been plagued by extreme nervous tension and that she feared
she would lose her reason. It also told that she went to see a famous
Boston physician. After a lengthy consultation, he had written the
following prescription: "My good woman, **you need to read your
Bible more!**"

Across the note relating this story were penciled her words: "*It
worked!*"

Have anxiety and tension put you on the sidelines? Are you suffering from dehydration of the spirit? Do you have anemia of the

soul? Read your Bible. "Thy word have I hid in mine heart, that I might not sin against thee."

Satan will fight! But keep on reading! Keep on drinking at Christ's well.

II. DON'T TRY TO LIVE A DAY WITHOUT PRAYER

Troubled Christians, don't try to live a day without prayer. As my heart contemplated this part of my message, three thoughts came to me.

1. *Anguish is best borne in prayer.* I thought of the anguished praying of Abraham in Genesis 18. I thought of Christ in the Garden of Gethsemane.

In your darkest hours, pray! In sickness, accident, tragedy—pray!

2. *Anguish is best borne when shared.* In Genesis 32:24 is the account of Jacob wrestling with a man. In Luke 24 the two disciples were with Christ on the road to Emmaus. In Acts 16 Paul and Silas are praying in jail—sharing.

A good pastor called me not long ago to say he was in difficulty. I talked with him, then prayed. He wanted to share his anguish.

3. *Anguish is best borne in service.* Give your all to Christ, as did David Livingstone, George Mueller, Adoniram Judson and others.

When George Truett accidentally killed a man in his early ministry, it changed his life. He bore his anguish in service.

A way to get rid of worry:

Contemplate the greatness of God. Think of His love and power. He is your Father.

Try to see His hand in all things—in the good and in the bad. Get a lesson for yourself.

Take everything to Him in prayer. Pray about the little as well as the big things. Oftentimes little things cause more worry than big things.

Don't cry alone! Pray—God hears and answers! You are not alone! Pray when you arise! Pray at every meal! Pray before you retire at night! Pray about everything! You are not alone!

"Be careful for nothing; but in every thing by prayer and supplica-

tion with thanksgiving let your requests be made known unto God. And the peace of God, which passeth all understanding, shall keep your hearts and minds through Christ Jesus."—Phil. 4:6, 7.

III. DON'T TRY TO LIVE A DAY WITHOUT REVIEW AND MEDITATION

Think of your salvation! By His grace are you saved. Think of answered prayer. Think of all God has done for you. Look back over your life. As you think of the past, you can see you were not alone. He was with you in trials, with you in suffering. Be grateful for all that God has done for you.

Often meditate on the goodness of God, on His salvation, His provision, His peace.

He is the One who cares for us: "Casting all your care upon him; for he careth for you" (I Pet. 5:7); the One who knows the answer to every problem; the One who will never leave nor forsake us.

Know your relationship. By faith you are God's child. Rejoice in your fellowship. Walk with Him. Maintain your service for Him. Work! God is watching over you! Don't cry alone! He will reward you!

Let's go back in history. The great Italian General Garibaldi freed his country from oppression. All Italy was made one nation. King Victor Emmanuel wanted to reward Garibaldi, but he firmly refused all rewards.

In November of 1860, Garibaldi made his way back to his humble farm, his homeplace. When he approached it, he recognized nothing. The rough, tangled farm had been transformed. There were roads, lawns, shrubbery—all elegant—but the farm cottage was gone. In its place was a villa replete with every convenience.

As he walked from room to room, he wondered who had made this transformation. Then when he saw a big full-length portrait of King Victor Emmanuel, he had the answer.

In the days of battle, he never thought of a reward. The big question was, "How can I serve my country?" He forgot himself! But the king did not forget.

My friends, our King (Christ) will not forget. Your future home is being made ready. The battle will then be over, and you will see all that Christ has made ready for you.

The imperative need is to *know* Him! to receive Him! And then the need is for each Christian to surrender to His will!

3   The King on His Knees

"And Hezekiah prayed unto the Lord. . . . "—Isa. 37:15.

It is a sure thing that all men need to pray! We are needy creatures, and we must have divine help. The extremities of life are too much for us to bear.

The sick person needs God's help; therefore, he must pray. The financially depleted need to pray; only God can help. The person with marital trouble needs to pray; his problems can only be solved and settled by the Lord.

Yes, all men need to pray: the poor, the rich, the noble, the ordinary, the old, the young, the up-and-out and the down-and-out. There are no exceptions—every person needs divine aid.

King Hezekiah prayed to God, and God gave a definite answer quickly. The Assyrians were encamped against Israel; but when the king prayed, the wheels of Heaven began to turn, and the answer of God was on its way.

King Sennacherib of Assyria came against Judah. King Hezekiah knew that he was coming to destroy the land as he had destroyed others; therefore, Hezekiah went before the Lord in prayer. Listen to his prayer as given in II Kings 19:15-19:

"And Hezekiah prayed before the Lord, and said, O Lord God of Israel, which dwellest between the cherubims, thou art the God, even thou alone, of all the kingdoms of the earth; thou hast made heaven and earth.

"Lord, bow down thine ear, and hear: open, Lord, thine eyes, and

see: and hear the words of Sennacherib, which hath sent him to reproach the living God.

"Of a truth, Lord, the kings of Assyria have destroyed the nations and their lands,

"And have cast their gods into the fire: for they were no gods, but the work of men's hands, wood and stone: therefore they have destroyed them.

"Now therefore, O Lord our God, I beseech thee, save thou us out of his hand, that all the kingdoms of the earth may know that thou art the Lord God, even thou only."

After such a fervent prayer from the king, did God give an answer? Yes. The promise soon came to Hezekiah through Isaiah, the prophet: "That which thou hast prayed to me against Sennacherib king of Assyria, I have heard."

The destruction of the Assyrian army we find in verse 35:

"And it came to pass that night, that the angel of the Lord went out, and smote in the camp of the Assyrians an hundred fourscore and five thousand: and when they arose early in the morning, behold, they were all dead corpses."

Let us study the prayer of King Hezekiah.

I. HE PRAYED BECAUSE THERE WAS A NEED

The king prayed—not just a poor, illiterate man in the back part of the kingdom; but the king went before God and laid the matter out before Him. Hezekiah went into the house of the Lord and spread before the Lord the great need, a need he knew only God could meet.

Thank God for needs which drive us to our knees! In this sad, self-sufficient day, so many feel they can carry their burdens by themselves. We have around us scores of failures—hundreds of men and women whose lives are vain and useless because they do not go to God in prayer.

Why do we fail to pray?

1. *We fail to pray because we think we are sufficient.* "We have

not because we ask not." Feeling the entire matter can be worked out in a satisfactory way by our own efforts, we turn from the business of prayer.

2. *We fail to pray because we are too busy.* Work and pleasure keep us from the most important occupation of all—fervent prayer.

It was Dr. Pierson who told the story of calling upon a clergyman who was laid on his back for six months. Dr. Pierson said to his friend, "You are a very busy man. It may be that God had something to say to you, but you were too busy to listen. So God had to lay you on your back so you might hear His voice and receive His message."

As Dr. Pierson was leaving the house, it struck him that he himself was a very busy man and did not give much time to listening to the voice of God. So he determined to practice what he preached. He said from that time on, "I have sat at the close of each day for an hour in the quiet of my study, not to speak to God, but to listen to what God has to say to me, and to lay the day's life and work open to the gaze of God."

Beware, my friend, of being so busy that you have no time to pray. Let it never be said of you that you do not pray because of your busy life. Take time to talk to God.

3. *We fail to pray because sin gets in the way.* The world, the flesh and the Devil conspire to keep us from prayer. When sin lays hold of a life, prayer vanishes. Yes, and when fervent, believing prayer takes hold of our lives, sin goes out.

Think on your needs and let them drive you to your knees.

Is it a financial or material need? Then bring it before the Lord and ask Him to guide you in this matter.

Is it a spiritual need? Then certainly seek His face. If you are a child of God but somehow not growing spiritually as you should, or you lack the peace which a Christian should have, bring it before the Lord and ask His help.

Is it the need of another? Then pray for this one. To pray for others is the greatest and best thing you can do for any person.

A minister was praying at the bedside of a dying woman. When he closed his prayer and started to rise, she said, "Wait a minute. I want to pray for you." Then very tenderly this dying woman prayed for him. When she had finished, she said, "For ten years, or ever since you became my pastor, I have offered that prayer for you every morning and night."

The minister went away with tears in his eyes and a strange warmth in his heart. He had known that this woman was sweet-spirited and true, but he had never guessed that he had a place in her prayers day and night.

My friends, let us not fail to bring the needs of others before the Lord. Pray for loved ones and friends by name. Mother, pray for your sons. Father, remember the needs of your children. Many a young person has been restrained from sin by the thought of his mother praying for him. Many a daughter has found it easy to be faithful because she remembered the voice of her father as he prayed for his children. We can offer prayer in behalf of those burdened down by the cares of this life, for God to give them strength and aid.

King Hezekiah prayed because there was a need. Let your needs drive you to fervent prayer.

II. HE PRAYED DEFINITELY

What was the prayer of King Hezekiah? He prayed for deliverance from Sennacherib. His prayer was not a review of his accomplishments nor a survey of God's grace and glory, nor was it a tirade against his fellowmen in Israel. His prayer was for help!

"Now therefore, O Lord our God, I beseech thee, save thou us out of his hand, that all the kingdoms of the earth may know that thou art the Lord God, even thou only."—Vs. 19.

The Bible urges us to be definite in our prayer. We are to ask, seek and knock. We are not to pray in general but in definite terms for the things we so sorely need.

A lot of prayer is good psychological exercise, but vain and useless. Why? Because it lacks definiteness.

The accomplishments of the Highland Park Baptist Church were brought to pass because of the definite prayers of God's people. Since 1942, when we first began, we saw God answering our prayers. Every phase of the work of this church was brought about because God's people prayed.

The mission program now reaches around the world. More missionaries are going out, and the work is constantly being increased.

Around us are chapels supported by Highland Park Baptist Church. As we worship each Sunday, they are worshiping, also. Some are small, while others are larger than 150 or 175 in attendance. This is the result of faithful prayer.

The Union Gospel Mission operates seven days a week. Men are given places to sleep every night and meals morning and evening. The cost of the mission is great, but God has supplied the need.

Camp Joy has been in operation for many years. Thousands of boys and girls have been blessed by the work of Camp Joy. The financial cost is great, but the results are greater. Souls are saved and lives are made over by the faithful work at Camp Joy.

The radio ministry has been going on since the second Sunday of December in 1942, the broadcast going into hundreds of homes in the tri-state area. Thousands have been reached through the ministry of radio.

But what has made all this what it is? The faithful praying of God's people here, joined by thousands in this area. Hundreds of people call in their requests for prayer.

The Evangelist paper has been going out for years, carrying the message of Christ into thousands of homes. The cost has been great, but God has supplied. What is the answer? Prayer.

The work of Tennessee Temple Schools is the result of prayer. The official vote was made by the church for the founding of the schools on July 3, 1946. Think, if you will, of the thousands of young people who have been touched and blessed by this ministry. Think of all those who will be touched in years to come, if our Lord tarries.

Hezekiah prayed. He had faith in God, and God gave His answer.

III. HE PRAYED IN FAITH BELIEVING

A blessed Scripture is found in Matthew 17:19, 20:

"Then came the disciples to Jesus apart, and said, Why could not we cast him out? And Jesus said unto them, Because of your unbelief: for verily I say unto you, If ye have faith as a grain of mustard seed,

ye shall say unto this mountain, Remove hence to yonder place; and it shall remove; and nothing shall be impossible unto you."

Hezekiah believed God. Can you not hear his voice as he cried, "Now therefore, O Lord our God, I beseech thee, save thou us out of his hand"? The answer from God was sure. Deliverance was given because Hezekiah prayed and believed the Lord.

Why shouldn't we believe? Has God ever failed? Pray in faith, believing. See the hand of God in every circumstance of life.

Sometimes the answer of the Lord may be greater than the answer we had anticipated or desired. For example, David lay on the ground all night and prayed for the recovery of that child of love and sin. But the prayer as he asked it was not answered. When the child died, David did not cease to pray and believe God. He comforted himself and said of the child, "I shall go to him, but he shall not return to me" (II Sam. 12:23).

The Apostle Paul knew how to pray—and he taught others the value of believing prayer. He besought the Lord three times that his grievous and painful thorn in the flesh be taken from him, but the thorn remained to pierce and harass him to the end of his days. Yet at the same time, God answered him this way when he prayed: "My grace is sufficient for thee."

The prayers of David and Paul were answered. Yes, God answers prayer. Pray in faith, believing, knowing that God will give that which is needful and best.

And now, we must come to the close of this message. Perhaps this question should be asked: "Who can call upon God's name?" The answer: The ones who can say, "Our Father." How do we become children of God? The answer is plainly given in John 1:12: "But as many as received him, to them gave he power to become the sons of God, even to them that believe on his name."

The first need for every person is salvation. After salvation we are to walk and talk with the Lord daily.

A man boasted that he had not omitted saying his prayers at night for seventy years. It pleased God to suddenly convert him at that age; then in a changed tone and spirit, he said, "I am the old man who said his prayers for seventy years, yet all that time I never prayed at all."

How true it is! The first need for every person is Jesus Christ. If you have not, will you trust Him as your personal Saviour now?

Daniel's "Aforetime"

"Now when Daniel knew that the writing was signed, he went into his house; and his windows being open in his chamber toward Jerusalem, he kneeled upon his knees three times a day, and prayed, and gave thanks before his God, as he did aforetime."—Dan. 6:10.

The prime minister of Babylon had trouble, but it was not a strange trouble. The authorities were mad at him. (Anger at leaders is not strange.) They were jealous of him because of his position with the king. He was preferred above the other presidents and princes.

Daniel was known as a man of God and of prayer. Therefore, his enemies talked the king into signing a decree.

"All the presidents of the kingdom, the governors, and the princes, the counsellers, and the captains, have consulted together to establish a royal statute, and to make a firm decree, that whosoever shall ask a petition of any God or man for thirty days, save of thee, O king, he shall be cast into the den of lions."—Dan. 6:7.

When Daniel heard about the writing, he went to his room and prayed as he had "aforetime." Daniel did not just begin to pray when trouble came; he continued as he had been used to doing—"aforetime," praying three times per day.

You might question Daniel, an official in the government, "Why do you pray?" His answer: "I believe in God. He invites me to come to Him with my problems. For years I have maintained the habit of prayer three times each day. Prayer gives me strength. The duties of my office are many, so I must pray. A praying man is forearmed for battle. I pray, for through prayer I have wisdom from God. I pray, for in this way I have fellowship with my God."

Daniel had sufferings—he had them. 'Yea, all who live godly shall suffer persecution.'

Daniel made supplication—he poured out his prayers to God.

Daniel had strength—he was upheld by the power of God. Praying people have unusual strength.

Daniel's secret—resting in the Lord. "Commit thy way unto him...."

I. THE PRAYING MAN IS WATCHFUL

The Devil does not catch him napping. The praying man is watchful for his own life. He protects his reputation. He guards against sin, for sin defeats prayer. "If I regard iniquity in my heart, the Lord will not hear me" (Ps. 66:18).

The praying man is watchful for his home. He desires the best for his family. He bars the door against evil through prayer. He leads his family in righteousness.

The praying man is watchful for his business. Dishonesty has no part with a praying man.

II. THE PRAYING MAN IS UNSELFISH

Daniel shows this. Abraham too was unselfish. Selfishness is of man; unselfishness is of God. True prayer and unselfishness walk together.

A praying man will tithe:

"Bring ye all the tithes into the storehouse, that there may be meat in mine house, and prove me now herewith, saith the Lord of hosts, if I will not open you the windows of heaven, and pour you out a blessing, that there shall not be room enough to receive it."—Mal. 3:10.

A praying man finds time to worship and time to help others.

A praying man will share his knowledge of Christ. I had a blessed experience today, leading a thirty-nine-year-old man to Christ.

III. THE PRAYING MAN IS GRATEFUL

"And he prayed and gave thanks before his God, as he did aforetime." Thanksgiving was a part of Daniel's life.

David constantly sang of his gratitude to God.

"Bless the Lord, O my soul: and all that is within me, bless his holy name."—Ps. 103:1.

"O give thanks unto the Lord; call upon his name: make known his deeds among the people."—Ps. 105:1.

"O give thanks unto the Lord, for he is good: for his mercy endureth for ever."—Ps. 107:1.

At the grave of Lazarus, Jesus began His prayer like this: "Father, I thank thee. . . ."

Be grateful! Thank God for your salvation and thank Him also for His promises.

IV. THE PRAYING MAN IS PREPARED

The praying man is prepared for life; he is prepared for battle; he is also prepared for death. Daniel was ready for the lions' den, for he had been praying daily.

Little prayer or no prayer means: tears, weakness, doubts (doubts come in when we let up in prayer), fears (fears stalk in when we let briars grow in the path of prayer), despondency, defeats.

No man is greater than his prayer life.

V. THE PRAYING MAN IS FAITHFUL

Prayer and faithfulness go together. Daniel was steady—a stalwart character. Opposition didn't change his faithful pattern. Any thinking person will soon arrive at the conclusion that the best life is the faithful life. ". . . be thou faithful unto death, and I will give thee a crown of life" (Rev. 2:10).

How the world shames us!

Mr. Al B. watches the "Today" show on television. He stands outside a window from 5:00 a.m. to 9:00 a.m.—rain or shine. At 9 o'clock he goes home, changes clothes and goes to work for twelve hours. Then he goes home to sleep so he can get up at 4 o'clock and be standing outside watching the television show at 5:00 a.m.

This man, grandfather up in his 60's, does three things: watches the "Today" show, works twelve hours, and sleeps five or six hours.

What an empty life! What dedication to nothing! How much better to be sold out to God! Be faithful!

WHAT ABOUT YOUR PRAYER LIFE?

The Crushed Heart Prays Best

"And Moses returned unto the Lord, and said, Oh, this people have sinned a great sin, and have made them gods of gold. Yet now, if thou wilt forgive their sin—; and if not, blot me, I pray thee, out of thy book which thou hast written."—Exod. 32:31, 32.

"But he himself went a day's journey into the wilderness, and came and sat down under a juniper tree: and he requested for himself that he might die; and said, It is enough; now, O Lord, take away my life; for I am not better than my fathers."—I Kings 19:4.

"Behold, O Lord; for I am in distress: my bowels are troubled; mine heart is turned within me; for I have grievously rebelled: abroad the sword bereaveth, at home there is as death."—Lam. 1:20.

"O Lord, thou hast pleaded the causes of my soul; thou hast redeemed my life. O Lord, thou hast seen my wrong: judge thou my cause."—Lam. 3:58, 59.

The disciples came to Jesus and requested, "Lord, teach us to pray, as John also taught his disciples" (Luke 11:1).

The Lord gave them the model prayer and followed it with the parable of the importunate friend.

"And he said unto them, Which of you shall have a friend, and shall go unto him at midnight, and say unto him, Friend, lend me three loaves;

"For a friend of mine in his journey is come to me, and I

have nothing to set before him?

"And he from within shall answer and say, Trouble me not: the door is now shut, and my children are with me in bed; I cannot rise and give thee.

"I say unto you, Though he will not rise and give him, because he is his friend, yet because of his importunity he will rise and give him as many as he needeth.

"And I say unto you, Ask, and it shall be given you; seek, and ye shall find; knock, and it shall be opened unto you.

"For every one that asketh receiveth; and he that seeketh findeth; and to him that knocketh it shall be opened."—Luke 11:5-10.

What is our Saviour emphasizing? The simple fact of our urgent need and God's response to the needy heart.

I find illustrations on almost every page of the Bible of my theme, "The Crushed Heart Prays Best." Illustrations come from the lives of Abraham, Jacob, Moses, David, Job, Elijah and Daniel, to name a few.

We need to know how to pray. The lessons may be painful, but they are needed.

Praying must not be a mere recitation of words; it must come from the heart. Don't be like the little boy who was used to sleeping with a night light on in his room. His parents decided that he was old enough to sleep in the dark. When Mother put out the light, he asked plaintively, "Must I sleep in the dark, Mommy?"

"Yes, darling," was the reply. "You are getting to be a big boy now."

The reply out of the darkness was, "Then may I get up and say my prayers over again—more carefully?"

Many of us pray carelessly. We recite words that do not come from the heart. We pray, but we pray without giving true consideration to our needs and to God's ability to answer us.

Three things I want to give in the body of this message. Each point will begin with a verse of Scripture.

I. "PRAY WITHOUT CEASING"

This verse, found in I Thessalonians 5:17, tells us that we are to pray at all times: in good seasons, in bad seasons; in prosperity; in depression. Always we are to be in the attitude of prayer. One of the hardest things for any Christian to do is to pray. Prayer is work!

1. *The world would turn us from prayer.* The politician has no interest in prayer. The business world has no concern in talking to God. The newspaper world has little interest in prayer. The social world cares not at all for prayer. If we follow the world, we will soon be turned from the place of prayer.

2. *The flesh has no interest in prayer.* These bodies have little concern for the spiritual. They are more concerned for the temporal, the earthly, the material.

A little girl, who had never been in church and had never joined in family devotions, was visiting her grandmother. On Sunday they went to church. The minister stood before the people and said, "And now, let us pray." People bowed their heads. When the little girl looked around and noticed all the faces turned toward the floor, she looked down for a moment, then asked, "Grandmother, what are we looking for?"

The world is concerned for itself. The flesh is interested only in that which will satisfy itself. Following the flesh will never lead to a life of prayer.

3. *The Devil is not in favor of prayer.* He doesn't mind a recitation of words, nor forms of prayer, but he vigorously fights against real prayer.

After Paul had told the church in Ephesus that they were fighting against the Devil, he then instructed, "Put on the whole armour of God." Then he wound up by saying, "Praying always with all prayer and supplication in the Spirit, and watching thereunto with all perseverance and supplication for all saints" (Eph. 6:18).

Satan will do all he can to stop you from praying. He will seek to interrupt you, to discourage you, to put you in such a rush that you will have no time to talk to God.

But now we come back to this exhortation given by the Apostle Paul, "Pray without ceasing." Be always in the attitude of prayer. At all times look to God for your needs.

II. "MEN OUGHT ALWAYS TO PRAY, AND NOT TO FAINT"
(Luke 18:1)

These words, given by the Lord Jesus, infer that life may have some crushing hours that might bring fainting.

1. *Sometimes the heart is crushed by suffering.* Many are the afflictions of these bodies. Hospitals and homes are filled with those with arthritis, tuberculosis, cancer, heart trouble, paralysis and a thousand other diseases.

One of the sweetest Christians I ever met was a dear preacher in Alabama, a preacher of unusual power. Then his voice failed completely. The church where I pastored bought him a loud speaker system, but it didn't work very well. When this man with a head full of knowledge and a heart full of love could not stand in the pulpit and preach, his heart was crushed. But after much prayer, God gave him the victory.

2. *Sometimes the heart is crushed by adversity, hardships, reverses and financial difficulties.* In such an hour, oh, it is imperative that we pray and not faint.

3. *Sometimes the heart is crushed by sorrow.* "There is no home without a hush." Sorrow has come or will come to every person. Most of us know its crushing effect. We know what it is to give up a loved one, to stand beside a casket. But I think most of us who have had this experience can also say with H. G. Spafford:

> When peace, like a river, attendeth my way,
>   When sorrows like sea billows roll;
> Whatever my lot, Thou hast taught me to say,
>   It is well, it is well with my soul.
>
> Though Satan should buffet, though trials should come,
>   Let this blest assurance control,
> That Christ has regarded my helpless estate,
>   And hath shed His own blood for my soul.

4. *Sometimes the heart is crushed by failure:* the failure of a

business, of your home, of a chosen career.

I picked up a man in Birmingham, Alabama, and he rode with me to Fairfield. This fine Christian man had a good position in Birmingham.

As we rode along, I noticed that he was excited and elated. His happiness was evident. Finally, I asked him what it was that was making him so exuberant. He answered, "I have worked at my present job for almost twenty years, and now comes the richest and best promotion I have ever had. I am to receive a judgeship, promised to me by some of the civic leaders. Happy am I that I am coming into this good place."

I rejoiced with him.

But I learned that the day he should have been promoted to that judgeship, the office was given to another.

This Christian man was driven to the depths of despair. His mind went bad, and he was sent away to an institution.

"Men ought always to pray, and not to faint."

5. *Sometimes the heart is crushed by hatred and animosity.* Hatred will come. People may hate you because of your convictions or because of your fervency in your Christian endeavors. Here is the lesson for you and for me: whatever comes, pray! Let every heartache draw you closer to Him.

III. "FOR EVEN HEREUNTO WERE YE CALLED: BECAUSE
CHRIST ALSO SUFFERED FOR US, LEAVING
US AN EXAMPLE, THAT YE SHOULD
FOLLOW HIS STEPS" (I Pet. 2:21).

As I make the assertion that "the crushed heart prays best," we consider our Saviour, and I call upon you to follow in His steps.

1. *Follow Him into the lonely places.* "And in the morning, rising up a great while before day, he went out, and departed into a solitary place, and there prayed" (Mark 1:35). "And when he had sent them away, he departed into a mountain to pray" (Mark 6:46).

We can and should pray with others at times, but don't forget the need to follow Christ into the solitary place and there to pray. In such a place we can bring before Him all of our needs, our weaknesses, our faults, our failures. There we can cry for the help needed.

2. *Follow Him to the graveside to pray.* Lazarus died. Jesus came to the home of Mary and Martha, and "Jesus wept." He then went out to the grave where Lazarus was buried. He told them to take away the stone from the place where the dead was laid. Jesus lifted up His eyes and said:

"Father, I thank thee that thou hast heard me. And I knew that thou hearest me always: but because of the people which stand by I said it, that they may believe that thou hast sent me."— John 11:41, 42.

In the sorrows of life, stay close by the Saviour's side. When you come to the graveside, feel His presence. When death takes away a loved one, have the assurance that He is weeping with you; then follow Him as you leave the graveside. Too many people neglect the Lord when they pull away from the cemetery. Oh, keep on following Christ!

3. *Follow Him to the Garden of Gethsemane.* Many hours in life we must fall down before the Heavenly Father and pray, "Thy will be done." Recognize His presence. He understands, He knows your need, and He can help you to the place of utter submission.

This present world is always seeking to lead us to a life that has no cares, no burdens. But all have discovered that life has its trials. The Bible proves so forcibly that the crushed heart prays best.

The crushed heart is driven to prayer. Where could Daniel go when his life was threatened? To the place of prayer. There he found God ready to help him, as in days gone by.

The crushed heart finds solace in prayer. We need and must have comfort. But comfort cannot be found in some psychological motto; it comes from the Heavenly Father.

The crushed heart is strengthened in prayer. When you come before the Lord and cry out, His help is ready. Though you feel so weak that you cannot stand alone, He strengthens you to fight the battle and win victories which in yourself are impossible.

The Anteroom of Powerful Prayer

"But thou, when thou prayest, enter into thy closet, and when thou hast shut thy door, pray to thy Father which is in secret; and thy Father which seeth in secret shall reward thee openly."—Matt. 6:6.

"Let us therefore come boldly unto the throne of grace, that we may obtain mercy, and find grace to help in time of need."—Heb. 4:16.

"Confess your faults one to another, and pray one for another, that ye may be healed. The effectual fervent prayer of a righteous man availeth much."—Jas. 5:16.

> **Take time to pray!**
> **When fears and foes distress you,**
> **And tiresome toils oppress you;**
> **Then the Master waits to bless you,**
> **If you'll take time to pray.**
>
> **Take time to pray!**
> **Come what there may**
> **To stand in the way.**
> **Look often to Jesus,**
> **And take time to pray.**

In this wicked, wretched day, man must have contact with God.

This is a day of wholesale compromises—compromises in homelife, social life, business life and governmental life.

This is a day of instability. Men shift from side to side, both politically and religiously. The mind of man is constantly under attack from the world, the flesh and the Devil.

This is a day of lessening morals. What is right? What is wrong?

Many laugh at the standards of the Bible. Immorality is accepted conduct in many places. Institutions of higher learning are becoming hopeless cellars of low living.

This is a day of religion. Everybody has a form of religion. Even Rabbi Sherman Wine has religion, though he openly declares, "I am an atheist." The Birmingham Temple, of which he is the rabbi, has grown from eight families to some 140, most of them young couples. One magazine, in reporting the rabbi, said, "The congregation generally finds Wine's godless, empirical approach inspiring." Says Attorney Merrill Miller, "He has made religion the most meaningful experience for me in terms of ethical and moral decisions."

The truth is, God hates religion. Religion crucified His Son. Religion has burned His martyrs at the stake. Religion has persecuted His followers down through the centuries.

We need prayer, for we daily need contact with God. In this message we are standing in the anteroom of powerful prayer. There are some things that must be settled, some things that we must understand if prayer is to be real.

It is like going to see an influential person. The secretary asks you to be seated in the outer office. It may be that you are going to see someone on business. While you sit there, you contemplate what you will say and what your approach will be.

It is this spirit in which I want us to sit in the anteroom of prayer. Some things need to be settled. May we consider three of them.

I. SETTLE SALVATION

Prayer belongs to the Christian. Prayer must be offered in His name. Why? First, He is the Saviour of lost man. The One who died for us holds the privilege of presenting our prayers to the Heavenly Father. Second, He tells us to pray in His name. But we cannot pray until we accept Him. Jesus said pointedly, "If ye shall ask any thing in my name, I will do it" (John 14:14). We must know Him. He must be our Saviour. Salvation must be a settled matter.

You can be as religious as Nicodemus, but you must know Christ to get your prayers answered. You can be as religious as Saul of Tarsus; but to get prayers answered, you must know Him personally and experientially. You can be as seeking as the Ethiopian eunuch; but to get prayers answered, you must know Christ as Saviour. You can be as good as Cornelius and offer prayers daily; but to get your prayers answered, you must know Him.

Settle salvation!

"But what saith it? The word is nigh thee, even in thy mouth, and in thy heart: that is, the word of faith, which we preach;

"That if thou shalt confess with thy mouth the Lord Jesus, and shalt believe in thine heart that God hath raised him from the dead, thou shalt be saved.

"For with the heart man believeth unto righteousness; and with the mouth confession is made unto salvation."—Rom. 10:8-10.

Let all doubts be removed! Believe that Christ is your Saviour. John tells us, "He that hath the Son hath life, and he that hath not the Son of God hath not life" (I John 5:12).

As we sit in the anteroom of prayer, we must first settle this matter of salvation. We must *know* that we have been born again.

II. SETTLE SIN

The sin question has ever been before us since the Garden of Eden. When we are saved, we are saved from the power of sin, but the presence of sin is still around us.

Salvation does much for us with regard to the sin question. It puts us in the family of God, gives us the indwelling Holy Spirit, opens the Bible to us, gives us a hatred for sin and an understanding of what sin is. If heeded, the indwelling Holy Spirit will intensify that understanding.

I speak now to the child of God. The sin question must be settled if prayer is to be answered. Let us consider a number of verses:

"If I regard iniquity in my heart, the Lord will not hear me."—Ps. 66:18.

"He that turneth away his ear from hearing the law, even his prayer shall be abomination."—Prov. 28:9.

"And when ye spread forth your hands, I will hide mine eyes from you: yea, when ye make many prayers, I will not hear: your hands are full of blood."—Isa. 1:15.

"Behold, the Lord's hand is not shortened, that it cannot save; neither his ear heavy, that it cannot hear: But your iniquities have separated between you and your God, and your sins have hid his face from you, that he will not hear."—Isa. 59:1, 2.

"Ye ask, and receive not, because ye ask amiss, that ye may consume it upon your lusts."—Jas. 4:3.

The Bible clearly tells us that sin must be settled. The saved one must be in the right relationship with the Lord before his prayers can be answered. Sin must be settled by confession, by forsaking sin, by the cleansing of the heart. This is exactly what John gives us in a familiar verse, I John 1:9: "If we confess our sins, he is faithful and just to forgive us our sins, and to cleanse us from all unrighteousness."

Our public altars need to be filled with folks getting right so their prayers can be answered. We want to pray effectively and see the answers; therefore, we must come before God confessing and forsaking our sins and receiving cleansing from Him.

Our private altars must also be occupied. We must come before God and renew our fellowship with Him. We must examine our hearts and turn from all wickedness and all sin, so that God can hear and bless our lives.

Now keep this in mind: when sin is settled, the answer is sure. When we pray for God's will to be done and in humble submission wait before Him, He will grant our requests. God is never too busy to answer prayer.

An army surgeon was once telling about an experience on the battlefield. He said after a terrible conflict, the ground was covered with the dead and wounded. There was work enough for twenty surgeons. It was doleful to hear their cries.

One cried out, "Doctor, I'm bleeding to death. Please bind up this artery." Another: "My limb is broken. Won't you take me to the hospital?" Another: "Doctor, I'm in awful pain. Can't you give me some medicine?" Cries were heard from all over the field. Certainly this was more than one doctor could handle. All were begging for help. A single army surgeon could not do the job.

Not so with our God! All cries will be heard. All prayers will be answered—when sin is settled and when lives are in harmony with His purpose and plan.

III. SETTLE SERVICE

First, settle salvation. Second, settle sin. Third, settle service. I speak now of the use of your life. Some things must be faced openly and frankly.

1. *Disobedient Christians cannot pray effectively.* Saul disobeyed God (I Sam. 15). Fellowship was broken between the king and the Heavenly Father. Saul followed his human reasoning and human desire and failed to utterly destroy the enemy. As a result, Samuel said:

"Hath the Lord as great delight in burnt offerings and sacrifices, as in obeying the voice of the Lord? Behold, to obey is better than sacrifice, and to hearken than the fat of rams. For rebellion is as the sin of witchcraft, and stubbornness is as iniquity and idolatry. Because thou hast rejected the word of the Lord, he hath also rejected thee from being king."—I Sam. 15:22, 23.

Open disobedience will sever the prayer line. When God gives you a task to do and you disobey Him, take the matter in your own hands, do it your own way, then God will not hear and answer your prayers.

2. *Unwilling Christians cannot pray.* Yes, they can pray for themselves, asking for forgiveness. And this they must do if fellowship is to be restored with God.

The best illustration of this is Jonah. God called him for a specific task. Unwilling to do what God said, he set sail to go from the presence of the Lord. God sent a storm. Jonah was tossed out into the sea; and from the belly of this fish, he cried to God.

First, Jonah was saying, "I will not." But when God finished with him, he was saying, "I will."

God may be calling you for some task; but if you are not willing to do it, then rest assured that you cannot get answers to your prayers. Man robs himself of ten thousand spiritual blessings because of his unwillingness of heart.

3. *Fearful Christians cannot pray—unless their fears drive them to God.* I trust I am understood in the beginning of this statement. We all have fears of one kind or another, but we must be believing when we make our prayers to the Lord. If we are doubting God and His Word, then nothing will happen. So believe God, put away your fears and trust Him to do what needs to be done.

Are you afraid to serve God? afraid that there will be some lack in your life? afraid that God cannot provide for you? afraid to speak for God? afraid that you might be embarrassed by someone or criticized? Are you afraid to stand for God? afraid of some criticism, some laughter?

O my friend, put away your fears and believe that in Christ you can do all things. Come before God in boldness and make your requests known to Him. You may tremble as you see the many obstacles before you, but don't doubt God. Believe that He is able.

A young sergeant, with tears in his eyes, came trembling to the great Emperor Napoleon and said, "General, we are hopelessly defeated. They have ten men to our one." Napoleon, straightening himself in his stirrups, said, "Put me down for 25,000. My skill, my ingenuity, is worth 25,000. We will be victorious." When the smoke of battle had cleared, Napoleon's army had won one of its greatest victories. The general knew how to tune his men for their greatest strength and most fierce fighting.

I use that illustration to point out that God has all power; and when you pray to our all-powerful God in faith, believing, then you can see great and mighty things happen.

Let us pause now in the anteroom of prayer. Settle salvation. Settle sin. Settle service.

"Hear, O Lord, when I cry with my voice: have mercy also upon me, and answer me."—Ps. 27:7.

7 The Prayers of a Singer

"Give ear to my prayer, O God; and hide not thyself from my supplication."—Ps. 55:1.

David is known as the sweet singer of Israel. His entire life as a boy, a king, a soldier, is as nothing compared to his songs given to us in the Psalms. The sweetest of the Psalms are simply prayers from the heart of David unto God.

By way of introduction, let us outline our thought in this way.

1. *David had a song.* His constant song was about God. He sang of God's might, God's love, God's grace, God's knowledge. He sang of God's concern for His own, of God's provision for the needy, of God's help in adversity.

David had a song that never grows old. Modern songs live for a few days, then die. At the very best, they exist for a few years, then are forgotten. But these songs of David have stood through all the ages.

2. *David had sorrows.* Songs and sorrows often go together. Knowing God was concerned about all things, he cried out his sorrows to Him: "Help, Lord; for the godly man ceaseth; for the faithful fail from among the children of men" (Ps. 12:1).

When he fled from King Saul, he poured out his heart unto God. Turn in your Bibles to Psalm 57:1. "Be merciful unto me, O God, be merciful unto me: for my soul trusteth in thee: yea, in the shadow of thy wings will I make my refuge, until these calamities be overpast." As you continue reading in this Psalm you will notice how

David cried to God in times of sorrow.

You will notice also that, when sin invaded his life, David cried to God. Psalm 51 is a picture of how sin had broken his heart, how sin had turned the song from the major to the minor key.

Watch out for sin. There is no sorrow like the sorrow sin brings. Sin kills the song. Sin hinders the singer. Sin hides the face of God. "And when ye spread forth your hands, I will hide mine eyes from you: yea, when ye make many prayers, I will not hear: your hands are full of blood" (Isa. 1:15).

3. *David made supplications.* The singing David was the praying David. Let us not quibble about how he prayed or where he prayed but how he made his supplication known to God. The Apostle Paul exhorts us in Ephesians 6:18, "Praying always with all prayer and supplication in the Spirit, and watching thereunto with all perseverance and supplication for all saints."

I will put this message under three simple headings in summing up the life of this singer who prayed.

I. TIME

Take time to pray!

> **Take time to be holy,**
> **Speak oft with thy Lord;**
> **Abide in Him always,**
> **And feed on His Word.**
> **Make friends of God's children;**
> **Help those who are weak;**
> **Forgetting in nothing**
> **His blessing to seek.**
>
> **Take time to be holy,**
> **Let Him be thy guide;**
> **And run not before Him,**
> **Whatever betide;**
> **In joy or in sorrow,**
> **Still follow thy Lord,**
> **And looking to Jesus,**
> **Still trust in His Word.**
>
> **Take time to be holy,**
> **Be calm in thy soul;**

**Each thought and each motive
Beneath His control;
Thus led by His Spirit
To fountains of love,
Thou soon shalt be fitted
For service above.**

Yes, David took time to pray, to express the longing of his heart. The Psalms record the fervency of his prayers.

We must give prayer first place in our lives.

Leaving the multitudes, our Saviour went out into the mountains to pray. He doubtless longed to be with His disciples, but more earnestly He wanted to be with His Father.

Prayer is not wedging in a few words of petition between your many daily activities—prayer must be a major activity of your life. Prayer must have a central place. Prayer accomplishes more than mighty armies. Prayer can defeat the march of communism, the progress of lukewarmness or the disaster of worldliness.

But we must pray:

"If my people, which are called by my name, shall humble themselves, and pray, and seek my face, and turn from their wicked ways; then will I hear from heaven, and will forgive their sin, and will heal their land."—II Chron. 7:14.

How should we pray? Perhaps we can give you an answer in just a few words.

1. *Pray in His name.* Jesus said, "If ye shall ask any thing in my name, I will do it." We have no righteousness of our own, but in Christ we can claim His blood-bought mercies and hold tight to the mercies He purchased for us on Calvary.

2. *Pray persistently.* It is not coming before God once in awhile and praying. It is appealing to the Heavenly Father, a constant communing with Him. The Son of God was often in prayer. He arose in the early morning hours. He prayed through the nights. He prayed persistently. So should we.

3. *Certainly, pray sincerely.* It is not turning a prayer wheel and saying, "Here are my prayers." It is not writing down a few words on a piece of paper and waving them in the face of the Lord. It is

coming before Him in sincerity and offering our prayers to Him.

4. *Certainly, pray humbly.* We cannot dictate to God. We must come in humility. James tells us, "Humble yourselves in the sight of the Lord, and he shall lift you up" (James 4:10). Don't dictate to the Almighty, nor tell Him how the requests are to be granted. Just pray and leave the matter in His hands.

5. *Then pray according to His divine will.* The prayer of our Lord from the Garden of Gethsemane shows us how we are to pray: "Father, not my will, but thine be done." God's will is always best for us.

6. *Pray with firm faith!* We are not to pray just when we have nothing else to do. We are to pray because we believe God and know He answers prayer. We believe His Word, and we rest upon the promises. We take very seriously His Word when He said, "Have faith in God," and also this Word of our Lord Jesus in Mark 11:24: "Therefore I say unto you, What things soever ye desire, when ye pray, believe that ye receive them, and ye shall have them."

7. *Pray everywhere: in church, in the home, on the street, in the business office.* Everywhere we go we should feel the need of prayer. Paul exhorts us to "pray every where."

Now to establish our hearts in this matter about prayer, let us read I John 5:14,15.

"And this is the confidence that we have in him, that, if we ask any thing according to his will, he heareth us: And if we know that he hear us, whatsoever we ask, we know that we have the petitions that we desired of him."

II. TROUBLE

"Be merciful unto me, O God: for man would swallow me up; he fighting daily oppresseth me."—Ps. 56:1.

"O God, thou hast cast us off, thou hast scattered us, thou hast been displeased; O turn thyself to us again."—Ps. 60:1.

"Hear my cry, O God; attend unto my prayer. From the end of the earth will I cry unto thee, when my heart is overwhelmed: lead me to the rock that is higher than I."—Ps. 61:1,2.

The Bible openly encourages us to come with every burden, with every care. The Apostle Peter declared, "Casting all your care upon him, for he careth for you" (I Pet. 5:7).

1. *Pray in the hour of need.* We are needy creatures. We cannot escape this. We have need of God's help, God's grace, God's provisions. There are hours of loneliness, hours of destitution, when we must wait upon God. How comforting is this word given by Paul, "But my God shall supply all your need according to his riches in glory by Christ Jesus" (Phil. 4:19). But remember, the supplies will not come unless we ask for them. If we turn a deaf ear to God and refuse His Word and way, then we cannot expect the supply of every need.

2. *Pray when others oppose you.* Make sure of your own position; then pray. Be confident that you are on God's side.

David never pretended he did not have opposition, never said he was without fear; but he did say, "What time I am afraid, I will trust in thee."

3. *Pray when sorrows overwhelm you.* In the hour of death, when shadows come on the home and in your life, then is the time to pray. It is then that you can say with real meaning, "The Lord is my shepherd; I shall not want. He maketh me to lie down in green pastures: he leadeth me beside the still waters."

4. *Pray when Satan seeks to trap you.* Remember, you are never away from Satan, never away from the Devil's power. He is constantly seeking to ruin you, to wreck your testimony, to steal from you the peace of God.

"Submit yourselves therefore to God. Resist the devil, and he will flee from you.

"Draw nigh to God, and he will draw nigh to you. Cleanse your hands, ye sinners; and purify your hearts, ye double minded.

"Be afflicted, and mourn, and weep: let your laughter be turned to mourning, and your joy to heaviness."—James 4:7,8,9.

Bible study and prayer are desperately needed when Satan comes against you. We ofttimes say, "Satan trembles when he sees the weakest saint upon his knees." The Devil will try to hinder you, try to keep you from service; but you can be victorious by simply resting in the Lord.

III. TRIUMPH

"I will love thee, O Lord, my strength.

"The Lord is my rock, and my fortress, and my deliverer; my God, my strength, in whom I will trust; my buckler, and the horn of my salvation, and my high tower.

"I will call upon the Lord, who is worthy to be praised: so shall I be saved from mine enemies.

"The sorrows of death compassed me, and the floods of ungodly men made me afraid.

"The sorrows of hell compassed me about: the snares of death prevented me.

"In my distress I called upon the Lord, and cried unto my God: he heard my voice out of his temple, and my cry came before him, even into his ears."—Ps. 18:1-6.

A blessed portion of the Word of God. When David won victories, he praised God.

I have always liked Psalm 37. In this Psalm David is giving us encouragement, telling us what to do so we might have victory:

"Trust in the Lord, and do good; so shalt thou dwell in the land, and verily thou shalt be fed.

"Delight thyself also in the Lord; and he shall give thee the desires of thine heart.

"Commit thy way unto the Lord; trust also in him; and he shall bring it to pass."—Ps. 37:3,4,5.

1. *The praying Christian will have victory!* It matters not what may be your trouble, if you will spend time in prayer, praying believingly, praying understandingly, then your own soul will know the meaning of true victory.

2. *Again, the praying Christian will have a song*—not a song in the minor key, but a song in a major key. Are you crushed by family

failures, household hardships or business reverses? Are you bowed down by the burden of broken homes, broken hearts, broken hopes? Then tell God all about it. Ask Him to take over and make all things new.

Do you know what it is to have victory in Christ? I am sure many of you can say yes. Do you know what it is to hear His reassuring words when your heart is broken? I know many of you can say yes.

When just a young man, I used to hear Dr. Carter Helm Jones preach. He had many good pastorates throughout the nation, but at one time was at First Baptist Church in Murfreesboro, Tennessee. He was one of the old-fashioned, southern orators. He combined dignity and sweetness.

I heard him speak one day in Louisville on "Roses in November." The message never left my mind. This is one of the sweetest stories he told.

> In my home in one of my pastorates was a prayer room—the Sky Room, we called it. It was in the very top of the house, a kind of attic room, and used only for prayer and meditation.
>
> One day, I came in, irritated and fretful. After I had been hurrying from one appointment to another, I told my wife I was going up to the Sky Room and not to let anybody interrupt me.
>
> She was always glad to see me go up to the Sky Room, for I was different when I came down. I dragged up the steps, shut the door and sat down by the little table. The only furniture there was a chair, a table and a Bible. As I idly turned the leaves of the Bible, I heard footsteps tapping on the stairway outside, then a timid knock.
>
> A bit irritated that somebody had slipped by my wife's vigil, I opened the door with a frown on my face to find my little six-year-old daughter standing there twisting her hands, because she knew she had disobeyed.
>
> "Daddy," she said, "you have been so busy these last few days that I haven't had time to love you, and I want to love you just a minute."
>
> I dropped to my knees. She put her little arms around my neck, kissed me, whispered something to me, then slipped out quietly.
>
> I just reached over and pushed the door shut without even getting up. I said, "God, I have been so busy going to and fro, up and down in the earth, that I haven't had time to love You

any. I want to stay here just a little while and talk to You."

My friends, our great need is to wait before God in prayer. In the midst of our tears, when nerves are on edge, when lives are tense and hearts disturbed—that is the time to pray.

It may be that you have allowed some sin to come into your life. Remember this: "The blood of Jesus Christ. . .cleanseth from all sin." Or if you have allowed some hard feeling to remain in your heart, then get rid of it. God will cleanse you and give you peace and joy in serving Him.

Prayer–and the Modern Home

"Peter therefore was kept in prison: but prayer was made without ceasing of the church unto God for him."—Acts 12:5.

In chapter 12 of Acts we read a story of persecution, prayer and deliverance. Few stories are as thrilling as the one found in this chapter.

Peter was cast into prison, but while there the people prayed for him.

The night before he was to be delivered to the people, Peter was sleeping between two soldiers, bound with two chains. The keepers of the prison were before the doors. It was then that an angel of the Lord came unto him. A light came down into the prison. The angel smote Peter on the side and raised him up quickly, saying, "Arise up quickly." The chains fell off from his hands. The angel told him to gird himself and bind on his sandals. This Peter did.

Peter thought it a dream and still felt that way until he had gone past the first and second wards and came to the iron gate that led into the city. At this place the angel departed from him. It was now that Peter said, "Now I know of a surety, that the Lord hath sent his angel, and hath delivered me out of the hand of Herod, and from all the expectation of the people of the Jews."

When he had considered this matter, he came to the house of Mary, the mother of John. In this place, many were praying together. He knocked at the door, and a girl named Rhoda came to answer. When she heard Peter's voice, she opened not the gate for gladness, but ran in and told how Peter stood before the gate.

The people said, "You are mad." Some said, "It is his angel." But Simon Peter kept on knocking. When they opened the door and saw him, they were astonished.

This story establishes a number of facts.

1. *People ought to pray.* Prayer is how to get things from God.

2. *It surely makes us see that God answers prayer.* We may feel that we are shut off from all help; but we are not shut off from God. When Peter was cast into prison, the people prayed for him. They might have gotten up a petition; they might have gone to the authorities; instead, they did the mightiest and best thing of all— they prayed for him.

3. *We are not as prepared for answers.* Rhoda heard the voice of Simon Peter, and with gladness she told the others that he was standing at the door. They did not believe that it was Peter and told Rhoda that she was mad. They said, "Why, it is an angel." They were not ready for the answer God had given them by releasing Peter from prison.

4. *Prayer should not be formal words but definite requests.*

These are but a few things that we see from this story in Acts 12. Now consider the place of prayer and the home.

I. WHOLEHEARTED PRAYER WILL MAKE A HOUSE INTO A HOME

Many of you have discovered this. Your house, once filled with unhappiness and dissatisfaction, is now filled with peace and joy because prayer changed the atmosphere there.

Christian homes are hard to find, even in this day when there are so many church members. Why? Because people seek to work out their problems by themselves instead of taking time to pray. It is easy to find houses where so-called Christian families live, but it is difficult to find true Christian homes where the Bible is read and prayer is offered.

Fervent prayer will change your home. At times when the home is engulfed by the affairs of the world, only one thing—the power of God—can straighten out your home problem. Prayer will do the job, so take time to pray.

Again, carelessness toward spiritual things will keep your house from being a true Christian home. Carelessness toward prayer, Bible study, worship and toward the house of God will rob your home of peace and joy.

Do you want a real Christian home? Then there are certain things that you must do.

1. *Pray earnestly and sincerely.* Let there be no sham about prayer. It must be real and earnest, or it is not prayer at all.

2. *Pray about all things—big and small matters.* Make no effort to work out serious problems by yourself, but bring them all to Jesus.

3. *Pray thankfully.* Let no Christian come to the table and partake of food without giving thanks. Put prayer first, both in your work and in your home.

> **Who without prayer, sits down to eat,**
> **And without thanks, then leaves the table;**
> **Tramples the gift of God with feet,**
> **And is like mule and ox in stable.**

Prayer will turn your house into a home.

II. BIBLE PRAYER WILL BRING MIRACLES

When Christians prayed in the house of Mary, the mother of John Mark, a miracle transpired. Simon Peter was brought out of prison. Great things always happen when prayer is fervently offered.

The Christians prayed, but notice that only Rhoda had faith to believe when Simon Peter stood at the gate. Rhoda means "rose," and this girl was a fragrant rose. Although she was doubtless only a servant girl, yet because of her faith, her name brings to us a sweet fragrance.

1. *Bible prayer will supply the needs of your home.* Our homes stand in need of spiritual blessings. It is prayer that will bring these supplies. Some homes have need of material blessings. It is by prayer that the needs will be supplied. Though you cannot see how the matter might be accomplished, God can. He simply waits on us to pray and to believe Him; then He goes into action for us.

2. *Bible prayer will bring the miracle of healing.* I have no right

to say that by simple prayer every sick person in your household will be healed; but I do say that, when people are ill, we should pray for them. In many cases, God has answered prayer and healed the sick. So we should ever be in close touch with Him so that, with readiness, we can call upon Him when there is a need.

3. *Bible prayer will restore family members who may have a wrong spirit toward each other.* Many homes are disrupted by dissension, arguments, backbiting and critical attitudes. Prayer can bring about a sweet spirit between family members. For this miracle, we can thank God.

Are you saying that certain affairs in your home are beyond repair? Then listen. Prayer will bring about miracles. Prayer will bring to pass that which you doubtless thought could never be accomplished.

III. HONEST, SINCERE PRAYER WILL KEEP OUT SINFUL AND OBNOXIOUS THINGS

Sin is knocking at every door. The world is seeking to inveigle its way into every heart. How can the home be made safe from the sin of the world? Only by prayer. The problems of separation are minor when people truly pray. The world will always seek to defeat a true Christian home, but when God's people pray, then things begin to happen. The trinity of evil is put to flight. And the Father, Son and Holy Spirit reign and rule in the heart and home.

Many of you can testify to the truth of what I am saying. Your home at one time was beset by sin and the world; but today it is beautiful, radiant and happy in the Spirit of Christ. What made the difference? Your faith in God, your acceptance of the Lord Jesus Christ and, certainly, your fervent prayers. Prayer became a power to defeat all looseness in living, all lightness in thought.

The home given over to the world is advertising that it does not spend time in prayer. The life beset by worldly attractions likewise tells us that there is no time spent with God.

IV. DEFINITE PRAYER WILL BRING SOULS TO THE SAVIOUR

Every true Christian will have an interest in others. If one does not have an interest in souls, there is serious doubt that he has ever been saved. The home that is not concerned about souls gives evidence that some who profess to be saved have never met the Master.

How shall we pray for others?

1. *Pray for them by name.* Calling their names to God and asking Him to touch their hearts will bring them to the Saviour.

2. *Pray faithfully for others.* By this I mean, honest, consistent, daily prayer in behalf of sinful mankind, those away from God. The Bible places a premium on faithful, not spasmodic, prayer.

3. *Pray for others fervently.* That is, pray with your whole heart. Pray so earnestly that you feel you will die if you do not see the answer.

Definite prayer is needed in soul winning. Definite prayer for your loved ones will produce the desired results.

But maybe there are some hindrances to your prayer. Perhaps you are wondering why you are not getting through to God. Allow me to point out some hindrances.

1. *There may be a wrong motive.* Turn to James 4:2,3:

"Ye lust, and have not: ye kill, and desire to have, and cannot obtain: ye fight and war, yet ye have not, because ye ask not. Ye ask, and receive not, because ye ask amiss, that ye may consume it upon your lusts."

A selfish purpose will defeat prayer every time. The motive in our praying should be for the glory of God and for the blessings that come to others.

2. *Sin is a hindrance to prayer.* Turn to Isaiah 59:1,2:

"Behold, the Lord's hand is not shortened, that it cannot save; neither his ear heavy, that it cannot hear: But your iniquities have separated between you and your God, and your sins have hid his face from you, that he will not hear."

This is a very distinct word regarding getting answers to prayer. Iniquity separates us from God. Sin hides His face from us. The trouble is not with God but with us.

3. *An unforgiving spirit hinders prayer.* In Mark 11:25, we read,

"And when ye stand praying, forgive, if you have ought against any: that your Father also which is in heaven may forgive you your trespasses."

An unforgiving spirit makes it impossible for God to answer our prayers. Do you desire the salvation of others? Have you been praying for someone around you, yet at the same time, maintained an unforgiving spirit? Read that verse again. God will not hear your prayers when you maintain the wrong spirit toward someone.

4. *Selfishness hinders prayer.* In Proverbs 21:13, we read, "Whoso stoppeth his ears at the cry of the poor, he also shall cry himself, but shall not be heard."

A selfish person cannot be mighty in prayer. Stinginess will shut the door and keep back great blessings.

5. *An unloving spirit hinders prayer.* Let us turn to I Peter 3:7 and read: "Likewise, ye husbands, dwell with them according to knowledge, giving honour unto the wife, as unto the weaker vessel, and as being heirs together of the grace of life; that your prayers be not hindered."

We are talking about hindrances to prayer. A very definite way to hinder prayer is by wrong treatment of a loved one.

Some of you may question why, when you pray, you are unable to get answers. Look into your own homelife. Husband, you may not be treating your wife like the Bible tells you to treat her. Wife, you may not be treating your husband like the Bible instructs you to do. Thus your prayer is hindered, and God withholds His blessing in the home.

May this be a time of dedication of heart and life to the matter of sincere Bible prayer. Let every Christian say, "As for me and my house, we will spend time in prayer."

The Deeper Meaning of Praying for Others

"I pray for them: I pray not for the world, but for them which thou hast given me; for they are thine."—John 17:9.

"Neither pray I for these alone, but for them also which shall believe on me through their word."—John 17:20.

If God answers prayer at all, then we know He answers prayers offered for others. The Bible is plain that the highest type prayer is that made in behalf of others.

So much of our praying concerns material things. It seems very little prayer is directed to the Father in behalf of needy ones around us.

As we come to discuss praying for others, remember that there are certain conditions to answered prayer.

1. *Plainly, we must pray in Christ's name.* "And whatsoever ye shall ask in my name, that will I do, that the Father may be glorified in the Son. If ye shall ask any thing in my name, I will do it" (John 14:13, 14). Keep in mind that Christ is our Advocate with the Father, our High Priest. We have no other way whereby to come into the Father's presence but through the name of Jesus Christ.

2. *Our prayer must be offered according to His will.* In the matter of praying for others, we stand upon a firm ground; for we know that it is the will of God to save sinners. It is also the will of the Heavenly Father for His children to grow in grace and in knowledge. It is the will of God for His followers to be turned away from sin and temptation, and to live righteously. Therefore, when we come to pray

for others and for their spiritual well-being, we can pray with real assurance; for the Word of God gives us a foundation upon which to stand.

3. *If our prayers are to reach the Father's ears, we must be in tune with Him.* Sin puts us out of tune. "If I regard iniquity in my heart, the Lord will not hear me" (Ps. 66:18). Isaiah the prophet said regarding Israel's sins, "Your iniquities have separated between you and your God, and your sins have hid his face from you, that he will not hear" (Isa. 59:2). Therefore, we need to make ourselves fit for this great work of praying for others. If we are really in dead earnest about helping our fellowmen, then we must be in earnest about preparing ourselves for the ministry of prayer.

Is it easy? No. Praying for others is never easy. We find opposition by the world, the flesh and the Devil. Satan seeks to hinder us, the world seeks to distract us, and the flesh clamors for first place in our prayers. Therefore, we must reckon with those who will try to turn us away from praying for others.

Now, what is the deeper meaning of praying for others?

I. IT MEANS TO FOLLOW OUR LORD

Christ, the Son of God, was a Man of prayer. He lived a life of prayer. He spent nights in prayer. He arose a great while before day. He sought the secret place to talk to the Father.

Perhaps you are wondering why the Saviour did this. Was He not the Son of God? Did He not enjoy unbroken communion with His Father? Yes. But as One who took upon Himself the form of a servant, He had need of contact with Heaven.

Christ lived a life of dependence. He rested upon His Heavenly Father. He knew that from Heaven must come His strength.

When will we learn this lesson: If we are to live a heavenly life on earth, we must receive power from Heaven?

Jesus prayed much. And certainly most of His praying was for others. Every prayer was unselfish. Every thought was to do the Father's will, to bring blessing to mankind.

Praying for others is Christlike. Jesus prayed for His disciples. Yes, and in John 17 we find that He prays for us. If we are to follow our Lord, then we must make it our business to pray for our loved ones and friends, yea, and for the whole world.

II. IN PRAYING FOR OTHERS, WE FOLLOW THE EXAMPLE OF GREAT BIBLE CHARACTERS

Abraham prayed for Sodom and for any righteous ones who might be found in that wicked city. His prayer was one of intercession.

Samuel prayed for his people Israel. The people came to him on one occasion and begged him to pray for them. His reply was, "Moreover as for me, God forbid that I should sin against the Lord in ceasing to pray for you: but I will teach you the good and the right way" (I Sam. 12:23).

The Apostle Paul prayed for others. He prayed for the churches and for the Christians that they might abide in the truth and walk with the Lord.

To the Romans, Paul wrote, "God is my witness...that without ceasing I make mention of you always in my prayers."

To the Corinthians, he said, "I thank my God always on your behalf, for the grace of God which is given you by Jesus Christ."

To the Ephesians, he said, "I...Cease not to give thanks for you, making mention of you in my prayers."

To the Philippians, he said, "I thank my God upon every remembrance of you, Always in every prayer of mine for you all making request with joy."

To the Colossians, he said, "We give thanks to God...praying always for you....For this cause we also, since the day we heard it, do not cease to pray for you...."

To the Thessalonians, he said, "We give thanks to God always for you all, making mention of you in our prayers."

To young Timothy, he said, "I thank God...that without ceasing, I have remembrance of thee in my prayers night and day."

To Philemon, he wrote, "I thank my God, making mention of thee always in my prayers."

From these verses you can easily see that the apostle was a man of prayer and that he considered it a part of his daily work to pray for others. He rejoiced in the salvation of souls, but he was concerned that Christians might grow in grace and in knowledge.

Paul knew that all things come from above. He knew that, if Christians were to progress, it would be because of earnest prayer on their behalf. Therefore, he prayed that those who had come to know Christ might be established in the Christian life. He desired that they would be stedfast, unmovable, always abounding in the work of the Lord.

He prayed that they might turn away from false doctrines and rejoice in the light of the Gospel. He wanted them to know the will of God and to love one another, even as Christ loved them.

To see also the importance Paul attached to intercessory prayer, notice that he requested prayer for himself. He wrote to the Romans:

"I beseech you, brethren, for the Lord Jesus Christ's sake, and for the love of the Spirit, that ye strive together with me in your prayers to God for me; That I may be delivered from them which do not believe in Judaea; and. . . may come unto you with joy by the will of God."

In the last chapter of the letter to the Ephesians, Paul said:

"Praying always with all prayer and supplication in the Spirit, and watching thereunto with all perseverance and supplication for all saints; And for me, that utterance may be given unto me, that I may open my mouth boldly, to make known the mystery of the gospel."

Yes, praying for others means to follow our Lord and the example of great men who were and are used of God. Outside of the Bible, we could name many others who were mighty in prayer, such as: Richard Baxter, who stained his study walls with his praying breath; Martin Luther, who did such mighty pleading that nations were brought to the foot of the cross; John Knox, who gathered up all Scotland in his arms; George Whitefield, who prayed so earnestly that thousands were brought to Christ; John Wesley, interceding for men until thousands had turned from sin to righteousness; Charles G. Finney, who prayed so faithfully that half of the nation was shaken by the impact of his life. Of course there are many others.

III. IN PRAYING FOR OTHERS, WE SHOW
CONCERN FOR OTHERS

The selfish person will pray but one prayer, one which I serious-ly doubt will receive an answer: "Lord, bless me." If selfishness is a sin—and it is—then selfishness will cause our prayers to go unheard.

If we love others, we will pray for them. We will be concerned, both for the saved and for the unsaved. Love will make us pray for Christians. We are all aware of the many around us for whom we ought to pray who are weak in faith, easily tempted by Satan and vacillating in life. Members of our own families stand in dire need of prayer. It is not enough to pray for sinners to be saved, and after salvation, desert them. We must continue to pray for our loved ones and friends after they are saved.

In a church such as this one, it is our duty to pray one for the other. I fear we are prone to criticize, and are not very active in pray-ing for each other. May this mistake be corrected, and may we begin to offer daily prayer in behalf of each other.

Many of our members are unstable. They are easily tossed about by every wind of doctrine. Their roots have not gone down deep into the Word of God. Other members have come to Christ out of lives of sin, such as drunkenness, drugs and gambling; these need our prayers that they continue steadfast.

Show your concern by praying for others. Make a prayer list of your Christian friends who stand in need of your support in prayer.

Pray also for the lost. Such did the Apostle Paul when he said, "My heart's desire and prayer to God for Israel is, that they might be saved." And again he said, "I have great heaviness and continual sorrow in my heart. For I could wish that myself were accursed from Christ for my brethren."

Make a prayer list of lost ones you want to see brought to the Saviour, and call their names to God regularly. Such praying will keep you unceasingly at it. It will make you a better witness, for no one can truly pray without also witnessing for Christ. If we pray earnestly for a lost one, we will want to speak a word to him or her about salvation.

Praying for others will also serve as a check on our own lives. A worldly Christian will not very long pray for someone else. He will be so conscious of his own deficiencies that he will either pray for himself to get right or else cease praying altogether.

We are entering a revival season. May the revival begin today as we begin to pray for others. Set your heart upon certain ones whom you want to see saved, and pray for them. Invite them to the church services. Witness to them. And wait on God for the results.

IV. WHEN PRAYING FOR OTHERS, WE ENGAGE IN AN ETERNAL WORK

That which is accomplished through prayer will stand for eternity. That which is done by the energy of the flesh will vanish overnight. When, through prayer, souls are convicted and brought to the Saviour, an eternal work is done.

Let us gain a new conception of what it means to pray. Let us see this as a great, mighty, eternal work which God has committed into our hands. Let us see that the strongholds of Satan can be shaken by prayer. Let us understand that more things are wrought by prayer than this world dreams of.

Pray with patience and faith. Pray persistently. Keep knocking at the door. Don't grow discouraged. Though days turn into weeks, and weeks into months, and months into years, keep on praying. Prayer is an eternal work and worthy of our greatest patience and persistence.

The Lord Jesus spoke much oftener to His disciples about praying than about preaching. In His farewell discourse, He said little about preaching, but much about the Holy Spirit and about asking whatsoever they would in His name.

When early Christians prayed, mighty things took place. If we would be like the first Christians and like Paul, then our first work must be intercessory prayer.

May we have the courage now to confess our sins and our failures in this regard. May we resolve to break through the clamor of pressing duties and give ourselves wholeheartedly to faithful prayer.

Revivals are the result of fervent prayer. Evangelistic campaigns, resulting in the salvation of many, come because of many prayers. Strong churches, generous givers, missionary volunteers, separated believers—all come as a result of prayer.

Perhaps you feel that your life is so weak and your failures are so many that you can never be used in this ministry. You need to be reminded that Jacob, the supplanter, became Israel, the prince. That which is impossible with men is possible with God. Lay hold upon the facts that you are indwelt by the Holy Spirit and that God desires to use you and that prayer is one of the mightiest forces in the universe.

Let us realize that this is the work God has given us to do, and be diligent in it.

Let us pray!

The Prayer Life of Jesus

"And in the morning, rising up a great while before day, he went out, and departed into a solitary place, and there prayed."—Mark 1:35.

(He prayed in the early morning hours.)

"And when she was come to her house, she found the devil gone out, and her daughter laid upon the bed."—Mark 7:30.

(He prayed for the sick.)

"And it came to pass in those days, that he went out into a mountain to pray, and continued all night in prayer to God."—Luke 6:12.

(He prayed all night.)

"Then were there brought unto him little children, that he should put his hands on them, and pray: and the disciples rebuked them."—Matt. 19:13.

(He prayed for little children.)

How much better to pray for them than rebuke them, as the disciples did. Everybody should love children, flowers and music.

"And he came out, and went, as he was wont, to the mount of Olives; and his disciples also followed him.

"And when he was at the place, he said unto them, Pray that ye enter not into temptation.

"And he was withdrawn from them about a stone's cast, and kneeled down, and prayed,

"Saying, Father, if thou be willing, remove this cup from me: nevertheless not my will, but thine, be done.

"And there appeared an angel unto him from heaven, strengthening him.

"And being in an agony he prayed more earnestly: and his sweat was as it were great drops of blood falling down to the ground.

"And when he rose up from prayer, and was come to his disciples, he found them sleeping for sorrow,

"And said unto them, Why sleep ye? rise and pray, lest ye enter into temptation."—Luke 22:39-46.

(He prayed in Gethsemane.)

Lonely, painful Gethsemane. In the garden: The lonely Christ, the humble Christ, the sorrowful Christ.

The greatest example of prayer is Christ. Christ, the Son of God, was a Man of prayer.

We all admire men and women of prayer. We like to read of the accomplishments of people of prayer. We are inspired to pray. We read of George Mueller, the man who supported great orphanages by simple, believing prayer. We read of the work of Praying John Hyde—an extraordinary man who stayed before God for days and weeks beseeching for miracles on the mission fields.

I think of the amazing life of Ernest Reveal of Evansville, Indiana. No books have been written about his prayer life, but it was astounding nevertheless. Miraculous answers came from his fervent prayers. Yet I recall something about Dr. Reveal's praying. He used the same tone of voice, the same expressions as when he talked to his friends. Talking to God was speaking to the best of friends.

Yes, others pray. I believe in prayer, but something hinders my prayer life. What is it?

1. *Much of the time I think I'm too busy.* So much to do, so little time to do it. This is a sorry and feeble excuse for failure to pray. Busier men than any of us have found time to pray, and so must we!

2. *Looking at others has often hindered my prayer life.* Their words, expressions and actions have stopped me in my prayers. It might be a sharp, critical word turned me from prayer. This should never be! My failures and the failures of others ought to drive me to

the secret place for prayer and a renewal of my life.

3. *Resting too much on the flesh has often hindered.* Depending on self to work out the problems of life instead of casting all my cares on Him!

4. *SIN—plain, old, dirty sin—has hindered my prayer life,* "If I regard iniquity in my heart, the Lord will not hear me" (Ps. 66:18). Sin—any sin—will hinder prayer. Sins of the flesh, sins of the mind, sins of heart—all sins hinder. How passionately we should hate sin! How we should run to Him for confession and forgiveness!

But, now, let us consider the prayer life of Jesus.

I. JESUS' PRAYER LIFE PICTURES A NEED

I speak so carefully! The Lord Jesus was the incarnate Son of God. This statement makes us almost shy away from the thought that Jesus could experience need in any way.

He was God-man as He walked among men. He hungered and He ate. He thirsted and He drank. He desired rest and He obtained it.

But by far the greatest need of our Saviour was His need of fellowship with God. He left Heaven's glory and came into this sinful world. He took upon Himself the form of sinful man (Phil. 2).

He needed fellowship with God, and He obtained it daily through prayer. Think of those early morning hours when Jesus prayed or the all-night prayer meetings He had with the Father! From the Father He received guidance, blessing and strength. All of this simply speaks to us of our need to pray.

1. *We need to have fellowship with God.* Life becomes painfully weak and miserably empty unless we can feel God's presence.

2. *We need guidance.* The labyrinth of a complex, sinful day is too much for us. We must have guidance—His guidance. Guidance does not come from radio, television or the press, but from God.

A few moments ago I looked through a Chicago paper. Page after page were stories of crime, death, burglaries, governmental uncertainties—nothing there to guide any stumbling life.

II. PRAYER LIFE OF JESUS EFFECTIVE

Our Saviour prayed, and God answered. He prayed for strength, and He obtained strength. He prayed in the Garden of Gethsemane, and the answer came. His sweat was as it were great drops of blood— His agony was so intense—but the answer came. The Heavenly Father even sent angels down to strengthen Him. The Saviour on trial is a sample of the effectiveness of His prayer.

His noble death on a cruel cross is another illustration of His effective praying.

Prayer must bring results! If not, it is a mockery.

We must believe in prayer just as our Saviour did. We have needs; we must pray for results. "If ye shall ask any thing in my name, I will do it" (John 14:14).

How sharply does James deal with this matter of effective praying! He said, "Ye have not, because ye ask not."

Today has been Inauguration Day in our nation. Great have been the celebrations in Washington. On yesterday I spoke to 175 ministers in Grand Rapids, Michigan. One of them bent over and whispered to me that President Lyndon B. Johnson had recently called Billy Graham and asked him to come to Washington and pray for him. This is good if the President will put away his bourbon, his dancing, profanity and a few more known sins.

III. PRAYER LIFE OF JESUS IMPRESSIVE

Jesus did nothing for impression's sake. But His disciples were impressed by His prayer life. They didn't enter too heartily into prayer as Jesus walked among them. Peter, James and John went to sleep on the Mount of Transfiguration and also in the Garden of Gethsemane. But they got the lesson. They could not escape it. Hence, we find prayer having a larger part in the ministry of the apostles from the ascension of Jesus to the end of their days.

They prayed before Pentecost and after Pentecost. They prayed in jails and out of jails. They prayed for Peter when he was incarcerated. When Paul and Silas had a midnight prayer meeting, God answered from Heaven with a mighty earthquake. Christ showed them the way, and they did not forget it.

He shows us the way to victory. The victorious Christian must pray. Victory is linked to faith and prayer.

IV. PRAYER LIFE OF JESUS SCRIPTURAL

Our Saviour prayed, as the Word exhorts us to pray. Abraham prayed. Moses prayed. Elijah prayed. David prayed. Daniel prayed. Our Saviour prayed more than the best of them.

Christ did not set up new patterns for prayer. He prayed as did men of old. He followed scriptural teachings and examples in His praying.

He prayed, "Thy will be done." No greater prayer could any man offer. This is the climax of all praying. The Father's will is always best. It was for our Saviour, though it took Him to Calvary's tree; it is for us, though it may take us through stormy, deep waters.

From my hotel room in a northern city, I watched men working on the construction of a large office building. I thought of the purchase of the land, the work of the president and stockholders. I thought of the getting of a building permit. I thought of the architect's planning, drawing, throwing away, redoing and, finally, presenting plans acceptable to the president and his board.

Then come the hours of meetings involving scores of men. Finally, the contracts are let on various aspects of the buildings.

The men lay out the ground. Men and trucks start hauling in concrete and steel. Work goes on!

I saw the building under construction. Big cranes were lifting steel. Men were crawling all over the building in zero weather! But every man had his job. The steel men, the electricians, the architects—all did their parts.

Down on the ground near the street was a lad with a job. His was putting canvas over some material. He fastened the canvas to the ground with bricks and chunks of concrete. Every man had his work! Every man was important to the task.

This illustrates the importance of every Christian and every Christian's prayer life. PRAY! SEEK GOD!

"Ask, and it shall be given you; seek, and ye shall find; knock, and it shall be opened unto you: For every one that asketh receiveth; and he that seeketh findeth; and to him that knocketh it shall be opened."—Matt. 7:7,8.

11 Mighty Power of Prayer

"Therefore I say unto you, What things soever ye desire, when ye pray, believe that ye receive them, and ye shall have them."—Mark 11:24.

"Confess your faults one to another, and pray one for another, that ye may be healed."—James 5:16a.

Next to the subject of eternal salvation, there is hardly any theme in the Bible which claims the attention of so many people as that of prayer.

Our favorite verses often deal with prayer. They are the verses which comfort and encourage us in the time of need.

"If ye shall ask any thing in my name, I will do it."—John 14:14.

"If ye abide in me, and my words abide in you, ye shall ask what ye will, and it shall be done unto you."—John 15:7.

"Be careful for nothing; but in every thing by prayer and supplication with thanksgiving let your requests be made known unto God. And the peace of God, which passeth all understanding, shall keep your hearts and minds through Christ Jesus."—Phil. 4:6,7.

These are but a few of the many verses which appeal to us and give us constant encouragement.

Our favorite Bible characters were men of prayer: Abraham, Nehemiah, Elijah, Jeremiah, Daniel and Paul. We are attracted to these men, not so much because of any deeds of greatness, but because of their faithfulness in prayer.

If we hear and read the names of great men since Bible days, we know of them primarily because of prayer. Our heroes are men who prayed mightily.

It is plain from the Word of God that there is effective and there is ineffective praying, praying that brings great results and praying that amounts to little or nothing.

Look again at the book of James. "Ye ask, and receive not, because ye ask amiss, that ye may consume it upon your lusts" (James 4:3). This indicates that some praying doesn't bring anything: "Ye ask, and receive not. . . ." James 5:16: "The effectual fervent prayer of a righteous man availeth much." This indicates that some praying does avail much.

There is believing praying and doubtful praying. If our prayers are to be answered, we cannot pray with misgivings, doubts and fears. We must ask in faith, nothing wavering, and believing God.

The difficulty is, we have taken prayer so lightly. We don't pray in great anxiety of soul. Prayer comes too easily for us. We pray at the drop of a hat, but it so often means nothing. Sometimes we must even confess that we are unable to pray. There is such a burden resting upon us, yet we know not how to pray as we ought. It is then that "the Spirit helpeth our infirmities."

Prayers that are offered so glibly and smoothly are not always effective. Beautiful prayers, couched in chosen alliterative words, do not always reach the throne of God. Quite often we must be so burdened as we come to pray for ourselves and for our needs that we are unable to find words to express our thoughts in audible prayer.

Prayer is work. Because of this, many turn away from it. This is not a praying age, but an age of hustle and bustle, of man's efforts and determination, an age when people are so busy, they have little time to spend with God.

We don't pray much in our churches. There has never been a time when we have had such beautiful buildings, such well-trained ministers, such a wealth of talent—all of it skillfully and thoroughly organized. But in spite of this, we can see the powerlessness of much we are doing. The Devil must be highly pleased when he sees all of our high-priced organizations, our million-dollar churches, our great choirs, big Sunday schools, but little power.

For this message I am turning away from some of the ordinary words about prayer, such as the fact that we must pray in the name of Jesus, according to His will, etc. Rather, I will deal briefly with three conditions for powerful prayer.

I. EFFECTIVE, MIGHTY PRAYING BACKED BY A GODLY LIFE

God doesn't change. He has the same power. He is able to do great and mighty things. But we are not able to pray mightily and effectively because we are not living as we should.

"Behold, the Lord's hand is not shortened, that it cannot save; neither his ear heavy, that it cannot hear: But your iniquities have separated between you and your God, and your sins have hid his face from you, that he will not hear."—Isa. 59:1,2.

To get ourselves on praying ground, we must turn away from every sin. There is a key that unlocks the storehouse of God's infinite grace and power. All that God has is at our disposal, but we must use the key of prayer.

1. *Sin hinders prayer*: "If I regard iniquity in my heart, the Lord will not hear me" (Ps. 66:18). When the Holy Spirit reveals sin to us, we must then confess it, forsake it and claim His forgiveness.

2. *An unforgiving spirit hinders prayer*:

"And when ye stand praying, forgive, if ye have ought against any: that your Father also which is in heaven may forgive you your trespasses. But if ye do not forgive, neither will your Father which is in heaven forgive your trespasses."—Mark 11:25,26.

Could it be that many prayers have gone unanswered which we have offered in behalf of lost loved ones simply because of our unforgiving spirit?

3. *A refusal to be reconciled to another will hinder prayer*:

"Therefore if thou bring thy gift to the altar, and there rememberest

that thy brother hath ought against thee; Leave there thy gift before the altar, and go thy way; first be reconciled to thy brother, and then come and offer thy gift."—Matt. 5:23, 24.

The Lord is saying that there is no use staying at prayer or worship if something is between us and our brother. We must first be reconciled to him; then we come and offer our gift to the Lord.

4. *Home relationships can affect prayer:* "Likewise, ye husbands, dwell with them according to knowledge, giving honour unto the wife, as unto the weaker vessel, and as being heirs together of the grace of life; that your prayers be not hindered" (I Pet. 3:7). Is there a right relationship in the home, an attitude of kindness, consideration and love? If the homelife is harsh and mean, then your prayers will go unanswered.

These are but a few of the verses which tell us that, to be effective and mighty, prayer must be backed by a godly life. A sinful, compromising life can never get results in prayer. Friendship with the world is enmity with God. To be a friend of God, we must be an enemy of the world and of sin. Every known sin must be quickly forsaken, if we are to have power.

II. PRAYER IS MIGHTY AND EFFECTIVE WHEN MADE UNCEASINGLY

Very plainly the Apostle Paul wrote to the church at Thessalonica, "Pray without ceasing" (I Thess. 5:17). For those who would argue with this statement, I suggest that the apostle means we are to live in a constant attitude of prayer. At every turn of the way we are to send up prayers unto God. The Lord Jesus put it in these words:

"Ask, and it shall be given you; seek, and ye shall find; knock, and it shall be opened unto you: For every one that asketh receiveth; and he that seeketh findeth; and to him that knocketh it shall be opened."—Matt. 7:7, 8.

He is encouraging us to keep on knocking at the door of prayer until it is opened.

Two very pointed parables were given by Jesus to illustrate

persistency in prayer. Though discouragements come, though adversities beset us, though Heaven be silent, we are to pray on and on and believe God.

The first strong parable is given in Luke 11. The disciples of John came to Jesus and said, "Lord, teach us to pray, as John also taught his disciples." Jesus gave them the model prayer. Then He gave them this parable recorded in Luke 11:5-8:

"And he said unto them, Which of you shall have a friend, and shall go unto him at midnight, and say unto him, Friend, lend me three loaves;

"For a friend of mine in his journey is come to me, and I have nothing to set before him?

"And he from within shall answer and say, Trouble me not: the door is now shut, and my children are with me in bed; I cannot rise and give thee.

"I say unto you, Though he will not rise and give him, because he is his friend, yet because of his importunity he will rise and give him as many as he needeth."

This parable teaches persistence in prayer. Jesus is saying that the answer is given when we keep on asking, seeking, knocking.

The second parable to which I call your attention is given by the Lord Jesus and recorded in Luke 18:1-5:

"And he spake a parable unto them to this end, that men ought always to pray, and not to faint;

"Saying, there was in a city a judge, which feared not God, neither regarded man:

"And there was a widow in that city; and she came unto him, saying, Avenge me of mine adversary.

"And he would not for a while: but afterward he said within himself, Though I fear not God, nor regard man;

"Yet because this widow troubleth me, I will avenge her, lest by her continual coming she weary me."

This parable teaches that we are to stick to the business of prayer, though everything may seem against us. The quitter wins nothing in this life. The person who wins keeps on just a little longer.

On the rock near the top of Mount Washington is a marker on the trail to show the spot where a woman climber lay down and died. On a clear day her action looks ridiculous. There is the top so close that you can almost hit it with a stone. One hundred steps more and she would have reached the hut at the summit, the shelter she sought. But this she did not know. Disheartened by the storm which beat on her body, she could not measure how far she had to go. She died one hundred steps from her goal.

A battle, the experts say, is won by the army which can hold out minutes longer than the foe. A man cannot do everything, but he can keep going. He has energy for one step more. He has a bit of resource left even when he thinks all is spent.

I repeat: the man who wins keeps going.

Here is another illustration to the point.

In 1916 the great Irish leader, Eamon de Balera, was arrested by the British in the midst of a speech to his constituency. He was taken off to England, sentenced to die, and relegated to Wakefield Prison, where he was to wait for his execution.

Such buffetings of fortune did not worry a man of his mettle. He went right on thinking about that speech, determined to finish it at some time or other.

As the world knows, de Balera was not executed. He was reprieved and escaped from prison. About a year later he was back in the Emerald Isle, and returned to the place where he had been arrested. Facing his constituency once again, he began with these words, "As I was saying, when I was so rudely interrupted...."

The quitter wins nothing in this world, and the quitter wins nothing from God. The victorious Christian prays on when others quit. He believes God when others think it cannot be done.

Mighty and effective prayer is made unceasingly and persistently before the throne of grace.

III. PRAYER IS MIGHTY AND EFFECTIVE WHEN OFFERED IN BEHALF OF A WORTHY CAUSE

Selfish praying is not heard. If we pray simply to satisfy our own selfish lusts, then the answer will not come. If we are praying to glorify ourselves, or to bolster our pride, then we receive nothing.

Spiteful praying is not effective. The one who prays to get even with someone else, or to get ahead of another, will get nothing from God.

Therefore, we must pray unselfishly, pray for the glory of God, and pray for the blessing of others.

What are some worthy causes for which we can pray?

1. *Pray for the work of Christ.* Christian, do you pray earnestly and daily for your church? Do you pray for the ministry of the church and for every department and division of the work? It is worthy praying to remember ministers of the Gospel in prayer. And pray for them by name.

2. *Pray for missions and for missionaries.* Let us never forget that missions is God's business; and as long as we stay in this field of prayer, God will shower down His blessings upon us.

It is a poor Christian who does not pray for missionaries. It is a poverty-stricken Christian who does not know the names of missionaries for whom he can pray. Let your life be saturated with the thought of missions and the need of the world, and pray daily for the work of missions and missionaries.

3. *Pray for the souls of men.* Remember in prayer those who are saved but may be cold or indifferent or disobedient. Within the circle of our families and acquaintances are many who profess to know Jesus Christ as Saviour, yet they are walking at a distance from Him. These people should be the objects of our daily petitions to God. Less nagging and more praying will bring more results to those who profess to know Christ, but are drifting along indifferently.

4. *Above all, pray for the unsaved.* How often do you pray for the lost? How many prayers go up for your own children? Wife, how often do you pray for your husband? How much time, children, do you spend in prayer for your unsaved parents? God delights in our fervent prayers for the salvation of others.

Two dear Christian people told me this week that they have prayer four times a day at their home. I can believe this easily, for to me the imprint of their prayer lives is upon their faces. It is also revealed in their faithfulness to the services of the church. Best of all, their effective praying is revealed in the members of their families.

Do you spend time praying for others? Do you have a prayer list, made up of the names of those who are heavy upon your hearts?

What a church you would have if all of its members would engage in daily prayer in behalf of its ministry! What tremendous results would be obtained if together all launched an avalanche of prayer daily toward the throne of God! If the effectual fervent prayer of a righteous man avails much, then how much could be accomplished by the effectual fervent prayers of many righteous people!

I plead with you to take hold anew of this matter of prayer. Let it become real and vital to you and a definite part of your daily life.

Let me review: Effective praying must be backed by a godly life. Prayer is effective when it is made unceasingly unto God. Prayer is effective and mighty when it is in behalf of a worthy cause.

Let us dedicate ourselves anew to praying. Let us determine to be prayer warriors. And let us be sure that we are praying effectively instead of wasting time in mere words which avail nothing.

And now, as we bow in prayer, let us join hearts in praying for the conviction and salvation of sinners who are in our midst. Let us pray also that God's children who are here will do that which the Spirit is directing them to do. May we be conscious of the power of prayer. Do not doubt that God can do great and wonderful things for us if we will pray in faith.

Building a Prayer Life

"And in the morning, rising up a great while before day, he went out, and departed into a solitary place, and there prayed."—Mark 1:35.

We cannot speak of prayer without remembering the prayer life of our Saviour, our supreme example in this important matter. Christ taught us to pray, but not only did He teach us regarding the importance of prayer; He prayed Himself.

In this brief message, I will give some suggestions on building a prayer life. Most of our praying has no foundation, no stability. We pray in spurts. We pray much for a few days or a few hours; then we skip prayer for a number of days. Prayer is vital to us at some times and a matter of indifference at other times.

I. TO BUILD A PRAYER LIFE, SETTLE CERTAIN IMPORTANT MATTERS

1. *Know that you are God's child.* To pray with confidence, you must be assured in your heart and by the witness of the Word that you have been redeemed. Through faith in Jesus Christ you have become a member of the family of God; therefore, you are enabled to pray, "Our Father, which art in heaven."

No adequate words can describe the vanity of prayer when an individual is not saved. There is something tragically pathetic about one's trying to pray when he does not know Jesus Christ as Saviour. His words are a clutching after that which he knows he needs, but he has no way of approach. He has no intercessor, no mediator, no

High Priest; he has absolutely no way of getting his prayer through to God. Therefore, the first essential is a knowledge that you are born again.

2. *Believe that prayer is a mighty force.* In short, believe that all worthwhile things are accomplished through prayer.

3. *Believe that God answers prayer.* So many people are in doubt about the efficacy of prayer. They wonder if the answers which they thought they received were mere coincidences.

Let this be established at once: God answers prayer! If He does not, the Bible is an account of vain fables; it exhorts us to do something extremely foolish and futile—if God does not answer prayer.

Be willing to meet certain God-given conditions for answered prayer. The prayer that moves the arm of God in your behalf is offered according to the conditions laid down in the Word. For example, prayer must be offered in the name of Jesus. It must be offered for the glory of God. Again, prayer, to be effective, must come from one who is right with God. The heart must be cleansed and in tune with God. "If I regard iniquity in my heart, the Lord will not hear me."

If God should hear the prayers of those who live contrary to His will and Word, He would be giving His blessing to sin and commending men in their sins. God cannot do this. The heart must be cleansed. The life must be right for prayer to reach the throne of God.

Now, when these important matters are settled, you stand upon a solid foundation when you come to pray. Prayer is not shouting out a couple of words in time of danger. Prayer is not calling upon God's name in an hour of panic. Bible prayer is based upon certain definite truths. Answers to prayer are given when conditions are met.

II. IN BUILDING A PRAYER LIFE, VIEW
PRAYER IN THE SCRIPTURAL LIGHT

1. *Prayer is a necessity.* It is quite apparent from the reading of the Gospels that prayer was a necessity with Jesus. If it was a necessity for the Son of God, then how much more is it a necessity for us.

Prayer is a necessity if we are to be in fellowship with God. What fellowship can we have with the Father if we never pause to pray? Fellowship with God is necessary if we are going to grow in grace and knowledge. We need fellowship like the earth needs sunshine and rain. We grow in the fellowship of our Lord by prayer.

Prayer is a necessity for victorious living. No person has ever gained great victory in life without prayer. David Brainerd was what he was because of prayer. Charles Finney was what he was because of prayer. Every outstanding, victorious Christian has been a person who spent much time in fervent prayer to God.

Prayer is a necessity for getting what we need. We all have needs. The promise of the Word is, "But my God shall supply all your need according to his riches in glory by Christ Jesus." The way whereby we tap the storehouse of God is to pray.

Prayer is a necessity if we are to help others. Yes, if we are to help others, either physically or spiritually, we must pray. George Mueller gave his life to helping orphan children, and he did so through the channel of prayer. He did not solicit funds, but he prayed. His life and work are perhaps the greatest illustration of prayer.

2. *Prayer is work.* It is not some fad or pastime or amusement. Prayer is definite work. If we fail to view it in this way, then we will soon become tired and weary in prayer. If it is work, then we must go at it with regularity. We must set ourselves to the task. We must give ourselves to it assiduously.

If prayer is work, we must go to prayer as a man goes to his job at seven o'clock in the morning. We must set ourselves to it like a carpenter sets himself to building a house, or as steel workers begin to build a bridge. The Bible and history give ample evidence that prayer is work.

3. *Prayer is warfare.* The Devil knows the power of prayer. He knows more about it than most Christians seem to know. He is aware that all of the world's greatest deeds have come through prayer.

The Devil fights those who pray. Here is the prime reason why you find it so hard to spend time in prayer. You know your need of prayer, you want to pray; but somehow you do not pray.

The Devil uses every method he can to distract you from prayer. Telephones, radios, motor cars, housework, children and television—

all of these things are used to turn people from prayer.

The Devil fights also to get you to put your faith in the flesh instead of in God. He makes you impatient; so instead of praying and waiting on God, you say a formal prayer and rush out to do a job in your own strength.

The Devil has proven himself successful in defeating Christians in the prayer warfare. It is easier to get people to give money than it is to get people to pray. It is far easier to get people to do physical labor than it is to get people to pray. Because of the Devil's awful power and work, perhaps the hardest thing to get a man to do is to get him to pray.

So if we are to build a prayer life, we must think of prayer as a necessity, a work, a warfare.

III. PRAY AT ALL SEASONS ABOUT EVERYTHING

"Pray without ceasing."—I Thess. 5:17.

"Be careful for nothing; but in every thing by prayer and supplication with thanksgiving let your requests be made known unto God. And the peace of God, which passeth all understanding, shall keep your hearts and minds through Christ Jesus."—Phil. 4:6, 7.

We should pray without ceasing, and we should pray about everything. Permit me to give some very practical suggestions.

1. *Pray many short prayers daily.* Those who pray successfully tell us that they pray again and again throughout the day. They pray as they work, pray as they drive, pray as they walk.

2. *Pray for long seasons about things which concern you.* Do you need guidance for your work? Then spend much time in prayer about it. Are you burdened for loved ones who are unsaved? Then set aside long seasons for prayer.

It was Praying John Hyde who locked himself in his room, stopping only at intervals to eat and sleep, and prayed three months for revival in India. How little we know of this kind of praying today!

3. *Pray big prayers.* By this I mean ask great things of God. Do not be ashamed to come before your Heavenly Father and make requests of Him for some big object. Be sure that you are doing it for

His glory. Be sure that self is in the background. Pray confidently for big things.

4. *Pray when you don't feel like it.* You will never build a prayer life on the changing emotions of your life. Pray at all seasons and about everything. There are so many times when you don't feel like praying—the Devil doesn't want you to feel like praying. At such a time, pray more than ever before.

When feeling defeated and depressed, that is the time to pray. When the body is tired and worn, pray. When feeling forsaken by God and man, surely you need to pray.

Pray and don't worry. "Casting all your care upon him; for he careth for you" (I Pet. 5:7). Christ urged His disciples to have faith in God. In the Sermon on the Mount, He spent much time in seeking to lift the eyes of His disciples Heavenward so they would trust in the Father. Chapter 6 of Matthew closes with these words:

"But seek ye first the kingdom of God, and his righteousness; and all these things shall be added unto you. Take therefore no thought for the morrow: for the morrow shall take thought for the things of itself. Sufficient unto the day is the evil thereof."

I was greatly interested in a touching story which I read in an English magazine. It was entitled, "How much does a prayer weigh?" The writer said:

> The only man I ever heard of who tried to weigh one still does not know.
>
> Once upon a time he thought he did. That was when he owned a little grocery store on the west side. It was a week before Christmas after World War I. A tired looking woman came into the store and asked him for enough food to make up a Christmas dinner for her children. He asked her how much she could afford to spend.
>
> She answered, "My husband didn't come back. I have nothing to offer but a little prayer."
>
> This man confesses that he was not very sentimental in those days. A grocery store could not be run like a bread line.
>
> So he said, "Write it on paper," and turned about his business.
>
> To his surprise, the woman pulled a piece of paper from her

pocket and handed it to him over the counter. She said, "I did that during the night, watching over my sick baby."

The grocer took the paper before he could recover from his surprise; then he regretted having done so, for what could he do with it? What could he say?

Then an idea suddenly came to him. He placed the paper without even reading the prayer on the weight side of his old-fashioned scales. He said, "We shall see how much food this is worth."

To his astonishment, the scale would not go down when he put a loaf of bread on the other side. To his confusion and embarrassment, it would not go down though he kept on adding food—anything he could lay his hands on quickly, because people were watching.

He tried to be gruff, but he was making a bad job of it. His face got red, and it made him angry to be flustered.

So finally he said, "Well, that's all the scales will hold anyway. Here is a bag. You will have to put it in yourself. I am busy."

With what sounded like a gasp or a little sob, she took the bag and started packing in the food, wiping her eyes on her sleeve every time her arms were free to do so. He tried not to look, but he couldn't help seeing that he had given her a pretty big bag and that it was not quite full. So he tossed a large cheese down the counter, but he did not say anything. Nor did he see the timid smile of grateful understanding which glistened in her moist eyes at this final betrayal of the grocer's crusty exterior.

When the woman had gone, he went to look at the scales, scratching his head and shaking it in puzzlement. Then he found the solution. The scales were broken. But as the years passed, he often thought of it and wondered if that really was the solution. Why did the woman already have the prayer written to satisfy his unpremeditated demand? Why did she come at exactly the right time when the scale was broken? What confused him so that he did not notice it and kept piling on the food with only a scrap of paper in the weight pan? He had felt like a fool and hardly knew what he was doing.

The grocer is an old man now. His head is white, but he still scratches it in the same place and shakes it slowly back and forth with the same puzzled expression. He never saw the woman again, and come to think of it, he had never seen her before either. Yet, for the rest of his life, he remembered her better than any other woman in the world and thought of her more often.

He knew it had not been just his imagination, for he still had the slip of paper upon which the woman's prayer had been written: "Please, Lord, give us this day our daily bread."

Oh, that we might pray and not worry! Look to God to supply your every need. Believe in the Heavenly Father. Stand upon a firm foundation when you pray. And have faith in God.

5. *Pray for others.* This is intercessory prayer. We should pray for many people. Our prayer list should be long.

Add names when you become concerned about certain ones.

I have tried for years to keep an active, up-to-date prayer list. I confess that I fail. I can see easily that this is the Devil's work. He does not want me to pray for others. When I have fervently prayed for people, I have seen remarkable results. But the Devil would see to it that the prayer list will get pushed aside.

I am resolved that I will make a new beginning this very day, that I will pray daily for certain individuals. For some I may not pray every day, but I will pray as often as I can.

What would happen if all of us in this room had a prayer list of fifty names, and each day we called these names out to God? Tremendous results would come in the salvation of souls, in the rededication of lives, in the calling out of young people into the Lord's service.

The successful prayer life must be built upon a deep interest for people. Love folks. Desire their salvation. And pray for them with great earnestness.

These are suggestions on building a successful prayer life. I trust that we will all profit from these simple words and that we start to pray without ceasing.

The Prayer That Availeth Much

"The effectual fervent prayer of a righteous man availeth much."—James 5:16.

"And it came to pass, when I heard these words, that I sat down and wept, and mourned certain days, and fasted, and prayed before the God of heaven."—Neh. 1:4.

For this message, please turn to the book of Nehemiah. We will follow the steps of one of God's greatest men.

1. *Nehemiah had great character.* He was noble, unafraid, loyal to God and to the people of God. There was about this man a strength of character which is lacking in most people of today.

It was Spurgeon who said:

> A good character is the best tombstone. Those who loved you and were helped by you will remember you when forget-me-nots are withered. Carve your name on hearts, not on marble.

It was Daniel Webster who said:

> If you work upon marble, it will perish. If we work upon brass, time will efface it. If we rear temples, they will crumble into dust. But, if we work upon immortal minds, if we imbue them with high principles, with a just fear of God and love of their fellowmen, we engrave on those tablets something which not time can efface, but which will brighten all eternity.

So it is that Nehemiah's name remains to this hour. He was a man of character. He was unafraid and loyal. May these characteristics also be found in our lives.

2. *Nehemiah had great compassion.* When he heard of the destitution of Jerusalem, he wept over the city and the needs of the people. His heart was often moved by the needs of others.

Compassion should be one of the first characteristics of every man and woman. If we do not care for others, then we will not be following our Saviour. Jesus was always concerned for those around Him. He had a heart of compassion. It was compassion which brought Him to the cross of Calvary. It is the great compassionate heart of Jesus which weeps over men today. This man Nehemiah had great compassion and manifested such by his actions.

3. *Nehemiah had great concentration.* When he learned of the destitution of Jerusalem and the needs of the people, he could not forget it. He concentrated upon the main task until the job was done.

Some people will never achieve much in this world because they attempt too many things. For my ministry, I have had only one interest, and that is the winning of souls to Jesus Christ. Perhaps someone is saying, "What about Tennessee Temple Schools which you founded?" My dear friend, the sole purpose of our schools was then and is now to train young people to be better witnesses for our Saviour and more effective in the spread of the Gospel. It is because of concentration upon the main task that we have buses, chapels and missionaries.

4. *Last, Nehemiah was a man of prayer.* Much could be said today about his ability as a leader, but I believe the main emphasis should be upon that which was first in his life—prayer. It was by prayer that he left Babylon. It was by prayer that he began the work of rebuilding the walls of Jerusalem. It was by prayer that he saw the job done.

Now, may we notice a few things about Nehemiah.

I. PRAYER AND TROUBLE

"And it came to pass, when I heard these words, that I sat down and wept, and mourned certain days, and fasted, and prayed before the God of heaven."—Neh. 1:4.

In the time of trouble, when his heart was moved, Nehemiah did that which should be natural for every child of God—he hastened to the place of prayer and waited upon God. Nehemiah had heard of the destitution in the city of Jerusalem. The trouble of his own people bore upon his heart. Unable to escape the burden, he prayed.

1. *When in trouble, always pray.* The Word of God tells us to pray without ceasing. This may not seem easy, but it is the way to accomplish the job for God. Have you been surrounded by trouble and difficulty? Did you look to God and pray?

2. *When in trouble, expect help.* We are most foolish if we think we can bear the burden and win the victory by ourselves. In the hour of trouble, look to God for definite help, and this help will be given. In the Psalms of David, notice how he cried to the Lord for assistance. Notice also the many Psalms when he gave thanks for God's help in time of trouble. David could say, "The eyes of the Lord are upon the righteous, and his ears are open unto their cry" (Ps. 34:15).

3. *When in trouble, do right and wait on God.* No trouble can be straightened out by wrongdoing. No difficulty can be solved by wrong methods. Wait upon God and do that which is right in His sight.

When Nehemiah was troubled, he went to God in prayer. As a consequence, he received permission to return to Jerusalem and to do the work which God had placed upon his heart.

II. PRAYER AND WORK

"Hear, O our God; for we are despised: and turn their reproach upon their own head, and give them for a prey in the land of captivity:

"And cover not their iniquity, and let not their sin be blotted out from before thee: for they have provoked thee to anger before the builders.

"So built we the wall; and all the wall was joined together unto the half thereof: for the people had a mind to work."—Neh. 4:4-6.

Will opposition come to the work of God? Yes. Expect it. It came to Nehemiah, to Moses, to Elijah, to Paul, to John and to other men; but there is victory through prayer. When opposition comes, pray.

Nehemiah knew that there was work to be done. He knew that the opposition could hinder this work, but he determined to go forward and do the job God had placed upon him. Therefore, we find in this man the combination of prayer and work.

Not only pray when opposition comes, but work when opposition threatens to hinder the program of God. It is a great thing to keep busy and to keep moving. All of the servants of God mentioned in the Bible were men of activity. All were not well in body, but they were active in the work of the Saviour.

Did the Apostle Paul have opposition? Yes. He faced it at every turn, but he pressed forward in the work which God had laid upon him. In the time of discouragement, the apostle worked. When it seemed that only failure could come as a result of his efforts, he still gave himself to his work.

Again, as you pray, work with a will. "For the people had a mind to work." The wall of Jerusalem was built by Nehemiah and his helpers because the people wanted the job done. They had a will to do the task. Any hard job can be accomplished when God's people want to do it. There is no problem so great that cannot be solved when we have a will to work.

Sometimes we are prone to forget that the world's greatest things have been done by hard work. I was reading recently that Newton rewrote his *Chronology* fifteen times, and Gibbon rewrote his *Decline and Fall* nine times. It is easy for us to pick up a book and read it, but we miss the hard work entailed in the writing of it.

It is an easy thing for us to view a house, a bridge, a road; but remember—work is back of it.

It was Beecher who said:

> It is not work that kills men—it is worry. Work is healthy. You can hardly put more upon a man than he can bear. Worry is like rust upon the blade—it is not the revolution that destroys machinery, but the friction.

Christian, give yourself to hard work. Remember that God's blessing will be upon you as you work in the Spirit of Christ.

III. PRAYER AND POWER

"Remember me, O my God, for good."—Neh. 13:31.

Prayer and power cannot be divorced or separated.
What is the power we need?

1. *The power to live.* The Apostle Paul found this power in Jesus Christ. When he was an active persecutor of Christians, he had no

power; for he was working in the energy of the flesh. But when Christ took over, amazing and wonderful power became Paul's. It was because of this divine power that Paul could say, "I can do all things through Christ which strengtheneth me."

It was through earnest prayer and submission to the will of God that Paul received the power to live and to serve Christ. It is by divine power that we are enabled to conquer temptations. By the power of God, we can be victors in the conflict day by day.

2. *The power to witness.* The greatest thing that you can ever do is to tell others of Jesus Christ. The greatest honor that can ever be bestowed upon you will be for someone to call you a witness of our Saviour. Here is the promise of God to you and to every child of God:

"But ye shall receive power, after that the Holy Ghost is come upon you: and ye shall be witnesses unto me both in Jerusalem, and in all Judaea, and in Samaria, and unto the uttermost part of the earth."— Acts 1:8.

There is no power without submission to the will of God. There is no power unless we are willing to witness for our Saviour.

Nehemiah had trouble. He had work, but he had divine power. This power can be yours also by submission to the will of God.

Perhaps I am talking to someone who has never accepted Jesus Christ as Saviour. My friend, life is vain, empty and fruitless without Him. He can give peace, satisfaction and joy. I invite you to come to Him now.

After the close of the First World War, a father went down to the station to meet his son. They greeted each other as only a father and son do after a long separation. They drove to the edge of the town where the soldier boy was given an emotional welcome by his mother and sisters. But after a brief visit, all the family retired to another room, leaving the soldier alone.

Confusion came over him. He wondered within himself, *Why have they left me? This is the hour I have dreamed about. I have been living for the day when I could come home; now that I am home, they have left me.*

He called to his father and asked him to bring the family back to the living room. They came. But they did not sit down. They stood in a semicircle. The son said, "Father, what is the meaning of this? Why did you leave me so soon after my return?"

Then the father began to speak. "Son, forgive us. We are all ashamed of ourselves. I hate to tell you, but, Son, you are not the way you were when you went away. Please forgive us for acting this way while we are getting used to you."

The son's face lighted up. He said, "Dad, is that what is bothering you? You mean because my body is not all here? All of you sit down while I tell you the most beautiful story you have ever heard."

I was out in No Man's Land. I had been cut down by shells and was lying on my back while a gentle rain fell on my face. My blood was mixing with the water and mud in No Man's Land while I lay there waiting for a hand to come out of the darkness and squeeze the last breath of life from me. I saw someone walking toward me. I could tell at a distance that his garments were as white as the new snow. He walked across No Man's Land as though it were a regal highway. He paid no attention to the shell holes, the barbed wire or the mud.

Almost at once He was standing by my side, looking down into my face. When He lifted His hands to command my attention, I saw they had been wounded by nails. When He spoke, His voice sounded like music in the hills at evening time. He said to me, " I am the Shepherd looking for My sheep that were lost. I am the King of all the kings and the Lord of all battlefields. I am the Resurrection and the Life. I am the Saviour of any man who will believe. I stand at the door of your heart and knock. If you will open, I will come in."

And then with a radiant voice, the son said:

I let Him in! I let Him in! He is there now. What difference can it make if my body is not all here? Someday soon I will have a body like His—perfect, indestructible and eternal.

My friend, will you come to Jesus now?

Prayer—the Open Door

"And he spake a parable unto them to this end, that men ought always to pray, and not to faint."—Luke 18:1.

The question might be asked, "Why pray?" The following answers will cover a part of the reason why.

1. *Pray because we need to pray.* We are weak, insignificant, needy creatures who must have divine help. Any person is fortunate who comes to the place where he sees his great need of prayer.

J. Edgar Hoover, once the head of the Federal Bureau of Investigation, said that a nation is at its best when it prays.

> The spectacle of a nation praying is more awe-inspiring than the explosion of an atomic bomb. The force of prayer is greater than any possible combination of man-made powers, because prayer is man's greatest means of tapping the infinite resources of God. Invoking by prayer the mercy and might of God is our most efficacious means of guaranteeing peace and security for the harrassed and helpless people of the earth.

2. *Prayer is Christlike.* Jesus prayed; we too need to pray. He taught us the need to pray. Don't fail to call upon God.

You have only to read the accounts of the Lord Jesus to see how He relied upon prayer for power and for strength. He prayed when He chose His disciples. He prayed on the cross of Calvary. Jesus prayed when people hated Him. He prayed for His enemies.

In a fit of anger, a man hurled a stone at his dog, striking the dog's leg and breaking it. The dog lay motionless for a moment; then he dragged himself to the feet of his master and licked the hand which had hurled the merciless stone.

For those who wounded Him, Jesus prayed, "Father, forgive them, for they know not what they do." Yes, it is Christlike to pray. This should be reason enough for spending time in prayer. Every child of God should desire to be like his Master.

3. *Prayer is commanded in the Bible.*

"Be careful for nothing; but in every thing by prayer and supplication with thanksgiving let your requests be made known unto God."—Phil. 4:6.

"Pray without ceasing."—I Thess. 5:17.

"Confess your faults one to another, and pray one for another, that ye may be healed. The effectual fervent prayer of a righteous man availeth much."—James 5:16.

These and many other verses tell us that we are to pray. Now consider three very simple things.

I. CONSIDER THE MAN WHO DOESN'T PRAY

What can we say about the one who turns from prayer and doesn't consider it important? When I speak of the child of God and his prayerlessness, I am referring to those whom we would normally think would spend time in prayer.

1. *He is afraid.* Fear comes in. But prayer takes away fear. Self-assurance, self-confidence cannot give peace of heart. The man who does not call upon God in prayer is afraid. He may have courage when the sun shines, but he is fearful in the shadows.

2. *He is uncertain.* He is uncertain about what he should do because he does not have divine directions. He is uncertain about the outcome of things for tomorrow because he is not relying upon the promises of God. No fear can depress a person more than the fear of uncertainty. The only way a Christian can have assurance that all is well is by spending time with God in prayer. Prayerlessness brings uncertainty.

3. *He is often consumed by worldly interest.* The love of money may consume his interest. A desire to "get ahead" may keep a man from going to God in prayer.

Pitiful indeed is the one who considers prayer a small thing. Nothing is so important to the Christian as prayer.

Do you consider prayerlessness a little sin? Listen! We are defeated by little sins—the sins that continue to accumulate in our lives until we are brought down and made ineffective servants.

A transatlantic liner was wrecked and sank along the Irish coast. There was no apparent reason for the loss of this great vessel. Divers were sent down to the wreckage to try to discover the cause of the accident. The compass was brought to the surface. Inside the compass box was found the point of a knife blade which had evidently broken off when some careless sailor was cleaning the compass. Only a little thing, but it drew the ship off course and caused the vessel to wreck.

Be careful that you do not consider prayer a small matter, for it is of chief importance for a child of God.

II. CONSIDER THE MAN WHO PRAYS

Many things might be said about the one who spends time in prayer. He is not pious and self-righteous, but is trusting and confident, knowing that God is with him.

1. *He is calm.* Yes, calm, but concerned. A picture of this is found in the ministry of the Apostle Paul. There was about him a great calmness, yet a concern for others. His mind was settled and quiet at all times, whether on land or sea. In the midst of a shipwreck, he could say, "Wherefore, sirs, be of good cheer; for I believe God, that it shall be even as it was told me" (Acts 27:25).

Paul was calm, yet always concerned for souls. In every place where he traveled, his first interest was in winning people to the Lord. His concern quite often brought opposition against him, but it changed him not one particle. He still had a concern for souls. Regarding his own people, he said,

"I say the truth in Christ, I lie not, my conscience also bearing me witness in the Holy Ghost,

"That I have great heaviness and continual sorrow in my heart.

"For I could wish that myself were accursed from Christ for my

brethren, my kinsmen according to the flesh."—Rom. 9:1-3.

Yes, the one who prays will be calm, yet concerned for others.

2. *He is assured—yet working.* Prayer gives confidence and assurance, not laziness. Nehemiah prayed, but he did not neglect working. Hear this verse in Nehemiah 4:9: "Nevertheless we made our prayer unto our God, and set a watch against them day and night, because of them."

Prayer gives us confidence when things are dark. Prayer keeps us moving forward when odds seem against us. Prayer gives calm assurance when others about us may be wavering.

3. *He is used of God.* Keep in mind that only a child of God can pray according to the Word. Keep in mind also that faithful, earnest prayer will produce definite results.

You cannot pray and remain quiet regarding our Saviour. You cannot pray—truly pray—unless you are aggressively engaged in work for Him.

Therefore, we can say with positive assurance that the one who prays is used of God. God uses us to encourage others. He will use us to do a work for Him. He will use us in the winning of souls.

III. FOR WHAT SHOULD WE PRAY?

Many things might be given, but I would like to summarize it all under three main headings.

1. *We should pray for the work of our Saviour around the world.* Jesus said to His disciples,

". . . the harvest truly is plenteous, but the labourers are few; Pray ye therefore the Lord of the harvest, that he will send forth labourers into his harvest."—Matt. 9:37, 38.

Prayer will bring blessings to the work of missions around the world. Prayer will get out men and women to the fields and prepare the fields for the harvest. This means that one of the chief needs in the work of missions is prayer. We have resorted so much to worldly methods of raising money and of doing the job, when we should be relying on our Lord, in faithful prayer calling upon Him to supply our needs.

In Dr. R. A. Torrey's message on "What Prayer Can Do for Churches, for the Nation and for All Nations," he mentions the following things that we should do in connection with foreign missions:

Pray for men and women just as the Word of our Lord Jesus commands us to pray. Pray for harvesters to enter into the fields, but there must be the right kind of workers to do the job God wants done.

Pray for the missionaries who have already gone out. Prayer makes the difference each day. Prayer makes witnessing effective. Every Christian at home should have some definite missionaries for whom he is constantly, persistently and intensely praying.

Pray for the outpouring of the Spirit on different fields. Oh, how much genuine revivals of religion in the power of the Holy Spirit are needed in the various missionary fields of the world!

Pray for the native converts. Torrey said:

> It is difficult for us to realize how many and how great are the obstacles put in the way of the native converts, standing steadfast in the new life, and the difficulties that lie in the way of his living such a life as a Christian ought to live in the atmosphere that he daily breathes.

Pray for the native churches. Pray not only for the converts as individuals, but for the churches as organizations. Every church has its peculiar problems. The Devil is seeking to defeat the work of Christ; and to do so, he works through the churches and causes division and dissension.

Pray for the secretaries and official members of various Boards here at home. One of the intentions of our missionary conference is to stir up interest in praying for the leaders of mission boards around the world.

Finally, pray for money. Many of the boards and missionary societies are in dire distress for funds today. There is need, and we should pray that those needs will be met.

Yes, pray earnestly for the work of our Saviour around the world. Remember to pray for laborers to be thrust out into the fields.

That was Dr. Torrey's list of things to pray about in connection with foreign missions.

2. *We should pray daily for our needs.* Do you have need of spiritual

blessing? a need of guidance? The Word of God tells us to ask, seek and knock. The song tells us:

> **If the world from you withhold**
> **Of its silver and its gold,**
> **And you have to get along with meager fare,**
> **Just remember in His Word**
> **How He feeds the little bird.**
> **Take your burden to the Lord and leave it there.**

3. *We should pray daily for souls.* This has been touched on in our emphasis on great missionary tasks, but I refer now to praying definitely for men and women to be saved, calling their names before God and asking Him to save them.

Revivals come when people pray. The greatest trouble with most of our present-day revivals is, they are man-made and not God-sent. They are worked up by advertising and special schemes, not prayed down. Pray for revival to strike our churches and our individual hearts. And pray for the salvation of souls.

This week a leader of young people gave me figures which he obtained from the F.B.I. office in Washington, D.C., figures obtained less than ten days ago. They are astounding as to the crime rate in our country, especially among the teenagers and juveniles.

We spend at least three times more on crime than on education. For every one dollar given to the Lord's work, ten dollars and more are spent on crime.

Recent figures will probably go much higher than these. The figures are shocking!

This should stir our hearts and cause us to work more for the salvation of souls. Pray constantly for others, that they might turn to the Saviour. Speak to men, women, boys and girls about the Lord Jesus. Prayer is good and effective, but prayer should be backed up by faithful witnessing.

> **Pray when the morning breaketh,**
> **Pray when the sun is high;**
> **Pray when the shadows falling**
> **Tell that the eve is nigh.**

Pray when the darkness deepens,
  Pray in the silent night;
Pray when the shadows, fleeing,
  Break into morning light.

Pray for the sorrow-laden,
  Pray for the tempted soul;
Pray for the saint, the faithful,
  Pressing toward the goal.

Pray for the missionaries,
  Calling beyond the deep;
Pray for the heathen millions—
  Over them pray and weep.

Pray that the truth, triumphant,
  Over the wrong may win;
Pray for the reign of power,
  Crushing the monster sin.

Pray, for the Bridegroom's coming
  Surely 'twill not be long;
Prayer then shall turn to shouting
  And to the victor's song.

Praying That Wins

"Howbeit this kind goeth not out but by prayer and fasting."—Matt. 17:21.

I am not interested in religious exercises! They annoy me, provoke me, and destroy within me that which should cry after the Lord. There may be a meaning to religious exercises (mere form of reading the Bible and praying or reciting creeds), but I don't know what it is.

1. *I am deeply interested in that which changes a man's heart and life.* I want to see a man come to the Lord Jesus Christ and trust Him as Saviour and enter into the relationship of a child of God. It is only by the new birth that men are made new creatures. This we find in II Corinthians 5:17: "Therefore if any man be in Christ, he is a new creature: old things are passed away; behold, all things are become new."

2. *A fervent study of the Bible will produce changes in the heart of anyone.* No one can study this Bible and continue in sin. Fervent, faithful study of the Word will produce cleansing.

"Wherewithal shall a young man cleanse his way? by taking heed thereto according to thy word.

"With my whole heart have I sought thee: O let me not wander from thy commandments.

"Thy word have I hid in mine heart, that I might not sin against thee."—Ps. 119:9-11.

It has been my experience to watch the changes wrought in lives when the Bible has been studied and followed. A critical reading of the Word will do nothing for you, but a faithful reading and a diligent searching will produce results.

3. *Earnest prayer makes changes in the hearts and lives of Christians.* Again we are faced with this fact: how many people pray earnestly, believingly? How many pray according to the Word of God? How many pray expecting definite answers from God? With many people, prayer is simply a habit, a recitation, a daily exercise that means nothing at all to the individual.

Too many of us pray as they did back in the first century when Peter was locked up in prison. The church made unceasing prayer to God for him. He was released. And when he came to the house where the people were praying, they thought it was an angel knocking at the door. Only when they looked into the face of Simon Peter did they recognize that God had answered their prayers.

Be not lacking in faith when you pray. Believe God and know that praying wins victories if you simply trust in Him.

4. *Dedication of your all to God will produce definite change in your life, your attitude, your home.* Notice I said a dedication of your all to God. We are beset in this day and time by too many who have partially surrendered to the Lord. They have not given all of their homes, their hearts, their lives, their aspirations, their desires, their possessions to Christ. All that you have must be given to Him, or else the great transforming change that He wants to make in you cannot take place.

Summing up: there must be salvation; second, a fervent study of the Word; third, prayer; and fourth, a dedication of your all to God, which means a willingness for God to lead and direct you in all ways.

Simply reforming doesn't mean a thing. I have listened to thousands of reformation stories. I have watched men turn from drink, profanity and loose living; but in a short time they were back at it again. Reformation doesn't make the change demanded by the Word of God, nor does it make the change which should be desired by every thinking person.

Joining a church doesn't change a man's heart unless that joining is accompanied by conversion and a change of heart toward God.

Too many have joined churches without joining Christ.

Pious talk doesn't mean a thing unless it is coming from a pious heart. The Pharisees could talk and pray piously, but their hearts were evil and adulterous. The Lord was angered by their shallowness. Like the surgeon's knife, His words cut into their hearts. Some were changed, yea, some saved; but many went their ways. I repeat: pious talk doesn't mean a thing unless it is coming from a pious heart.

We are coming to a discussion on the subject of prayer. If there is any place where a man could be wrong, it is in this matter of praying. Yet prayer is so important—no great spiritual life can be built without prayer.

The Word exhorts us to pray. We are exhorted by the examples of Christians in days gone by. We are exhorted by positive teachings of the Word. Such a one is given by Paul in Romans 12:12: "Rejoicing in hope; patient in tribulation; continuing instant in prayer."

Both by direct teachings on this subject and by the example of God's great people of days gone by, we have given to us the importance of prayer.

We must remember that our Master prayed. He was a man of prayer. Such a phrase as Luke 9:18 cannot fail to reach our hearts: "And it came to pass, as he was alone praying. . . ." Jesus "alone praying." Some people do not like to be alone because they have no delight in prayer. But Jesus often sought the place of solitude, so He might be alone with God, His Father, whom He loved.

This is what we must note: if the holy and sinless Jesus found it needful and blessed to pray in secret, how much more do we need to.

The Lord Jesus prayed at His baptism. He prayed on the Mount of Transfiguration. He prayed when He was choosing His disciples. He prayed when the Jews sought to kill Him. He prayed in the Garden of Gethsemane. He prayed from the cross of Calvary. If you are seeking for illustrations and exhortations on prayer, you can surely find them in the life of our Master.

The Apostle Paul prayed. Surely he had one of the greatest minds ever called upon to engage in the work of our Saviour. But, with humility, the apostle prayed. He sought the face of God and laid everything before Him.

Prayer is good! Everyone believes that it is good. We know that prayer works. Then the question, "Why don't we pray?"

Now we turn to the scriptural story before us.

I. NEED OF THE CHILD

"And when they were come to the multitude, there came to him a certain man, kneeling down to him, and saying, Lord, have mercy on my son: for he is lunatick, and sore vexed: for ofttimes he falleth into the fire, and oft into the water."—Matt. 17:14, 15.

With clarity the Word presents the burdened heart of the father. He came kneeling, begging, crying and beseeching for the Lord to do something for his boy.

This burdened father was not like the brute of a man who killed his eleven-month-old baby because the child cried and disturbed his television program, as told on the front page of the papers. No, this man had one desire—to get help for his boy. With crying and anxiety of heart he came before Jesus.

Thank God for the deep needs which drive us to His side! Satan would try to keep us from our Lord, but our needs drive us to Him.

1. *The needs of others should cause us to come to Him.* Our hearts should be moved by those around us who are in need. We should pray for them that they might be reached with the Gospel.

A God-fearing boy was reasoning with a sinful companion about his continuance in a wicked course. The boy answered, "It's all right for you, Harry, to be a Christian. You have lots of people who care about you. But as for me, nobody prays for me. No one thinks that I will do any good. They have given me up. They don't care." The Christian boy replied, "Jack, God is my witness, I don't lie down to sleep until I have prayed for your salvation, and I shall continue to do so until you accept Christ."

The heart of this friend was broken by the interest of his buddy. In a short time he had turned to the Saviour and was witnessing and testifying to the grace of God.

Let the needs of others be upon your hearts. Pray for them, and let them know you are praying for them. Make your prayer list. Keep it active.

2. *The need of our own hearts should drive us to His side.* As we sense a coldness coming in, we should come to the Lord in fervent prayer and pray about it. When we find a critical spirit taking over and causing us to depart from the place of service and usefulness, we should beware of it and confess it to the Lord and ask for His help.

The Lord is concerned about you and me. He wants to help us and stands ready to give aid whenever we call upon Him.

Now, let us keep before us the first point of this message—the need of the child. Here is a beseeching father and a poor boy whose mind was deranged, who caused great concern to his parents.

II. FAILURE OF THE DISCIPLES

"And I brought him to thy disciples, and they could not cure him."—Matt. 17:16.

1. *The disciples' failure to help him.* It is pointed out to us by the Saviour that they failed because they lacked in faith and would not pay the price to have power with God.

Has your life been denoted by failure? Have you failed to be used of God in the winning of others to Christ? Have you failed to turn the members of your family to the Lord? The first step to success must be an acknowledgment of failure.

2. *The rebuke of Christ.* The words of our Lord seem quite sharp to us as we read them.

"Then Jesus answered and said, O faithless and perverse generation, how long shall I be with you? how long shall I suffer you? bring him hither to me."—Vs. 17.

"And Jesus said unto them, Because of your unbelief: for verily I say unto you, If ye have faith as a grain of mustard seed, ye shall say unto this mountain, Remove hence to yonder place; and it shall remove; and nothing shall be impossible unto you."—Vs. 20.

No one can fail to see the sharpness of our Lord's words to His faithless disciples. They had failed, and Jesus pointed out why.

We confess today that we have often failed. The sting of our Lord's words comes to us in great power. We have failed in praying, in giving, in living. We have failed because we are faithless. We believe in Christ the Saviour, in God as Father; but somehow we have not prayed in faith believing. To us, Jesus would say, "Because of unbelief you do not have answers to your prayers."

We fail because we do not pray, and we fail because we do not pray aright.

We fail because we are following man, not God. A young man this week told of the difficulty he is having in his church. Some of the members are asking for his resignation, not because he has failed in his work, but because certain leaders of the Association feel it would be better if he were out of the situation. These poor, deluded men are following men and not God.

Our churches fail unless we pray. At a certain church, two men were being considered as pastor. Very little prayer was offered. There was much conversation. On the day the vote was to be taken, all the telephone lines were busy, but the line of prayer between the church members and God was idle.

That night the church took the vote after much quarreling and after many hard things had been said by the members. The man who won out by a very narrow margin accepted the call and came to the field. In a little while the church was torn to pieces. Large groups were pulling out to join other churches. The members were very unhappy, and the strong church became a weak church. Why? Because they failed to pray.

May the sting of our Saviour's words stay in our hearts until we can say we are going to do His will, whatever the cost. May we not fail because of lack in prayer. May we call upon God's name and seek His face and look to Him for divine blessings.

III. SUCCESS OF OUR SAVIOUR

"And Jesus rebuked the devil; and he departed out of him: and the child was cured from that very hour."—Vs. 18.

Christ succeeded! The disciples failed. Perhaps you are saying that this is to be expected, but our Saviour pointed out the reason for their failure. He said it was because of their unbelief. In plain words, the Lord is guaranteeing success in prayer for anyone who will pray in faith believing.

1. *There must be faith in God.* Jesus said, "If ye have faith as a grain of mustard seed, ye shall say unto this mountain, Remove hence to yonder place; and it shall remove, and nothing shall be impossible unto you."

When He rebuked the disciples, He said, "O faithless and perverse generation." What is the trouble? We know that God can do the work, but the difficulty is in our not having faith in God to do the job.

2. *Prayer and fasting.* Are you afraid of this statement of our Lord? Then wait! We will never get anywhere until the preeminence of prayer takes hold. This will mean such deep concern that prayer and fasting will be the results. I doubt that our Lord is teaching that we should force ourselves to pray or to fast; but when we have such deep concern for certain matters, we will both pray and fast until the job is done and the prayer is answered.

Someone has said, "Prayer and fasting form the two-edged sword that gets the victory. It is questionable if we really pray as we ought unless we esteem it better than our daily food."

The story is told of the woman who prayed quite faithfully for ten years for her unbelieving husband, yet she had failed to tell others of her burdened heart.

One evening at the church prayer meeting her heart was burdened more than usual. Near the close of the service she arose timidly and said, "For many years, dear friends, I have longed to ask you to help me to pray. I do not like to speak in public, but I can forbear no longer. Will you pray for my husband?"

Every heart was touched. Immediately they began to pray. One by one they prayed for the man of the community who was unsaved.

Just as the woman had made her request, her husband, as was his custom, came to the church to accompany her home. Finding that the services had not yet closed, he entered unobserved and took a seat near the door. When the service ended, he was waiting for her at the door.

As they walked away, he said, "Tell me, Wife, who was the gentleman they were praying for just now?"

She replied, "He is the husband of one of the ladies of the church."

When they reached their home, he asked again, "Who was it they were praying for?"

She replied again, "The husband of one of the ladies."

The unbelieving man said, "Well, Wife, that man will certainly be converted. I never heard such prayers before." Again, as they were getting ready to go to bed, he asked earnestly, "Those wonderful prayers, Wife—can you tell me the gentleman's name?"

She simply replied, "He was the husband of one of the ladies present." The wife went aside to pray again for the salvation of her husband.

At midnight she heard her husband's voice crying, "Wife! Wife! God heard those prayers. I cannot sleep, Wife. Will you pray for me? Can the Lord show mercy to me?"

That night the man was saved. When morning came, they called the pastor. When he arrived at the home, he found the man praising and blessing God.

The faithful praying of the wife, yes, and the united praying of God's people as they joined together in earnest prayer for the salvation of another, were heard and answered by God!

Around us we see the deep need of so many. We see the failure of many disciples and the success of our Lord. Whenever He comes into the picture and begins to work, things begin to happen!

Will you not resign yourself at this time to a life of devoted prayer? Pray in the secret place. Pray with others. Join in fervent prayer daily for God's blessings upon your life, your home, your loved ones, your friends.

There is a praying that wins—let us do that kind of praying.

16 The One Indispensable Prerequisite for Revival

"O Lord, I have heard thy speech, and was afraid: O Lord, revive thy work in the midst of the years, in the midst of the years make known; in wrath remember mercy."—Hab. 3:2.

"And it came to pass, that, as he was praying in a certain place, when he ceased, one of his disciples said unto him, Lord, teach us to pray, as John also taught his disciples."—Luke 11:1.

No one questions the importance of **preaching** in revival movements and revival meetings. There must be a clear and forceful presentation of the gospel message and a fearless condemnation of sin from the pulpit if revival is to come.

No one questions the importance of **singing** in a revival. Godly music blesses and inspires. Preaching and music have always gone together. The great revivals of days gone by have been characterized by fervent singing.

No one questions the importance of **witnessing** in revival. Every Christian needs to be a witness. When a revival is scheduled, we should make it our business to witness to many and to invite everyone we can to the revival effort.

No one questions the importance of **crowds** in revivals. They are essential to successful meetings. We cannot reach many unless many are brought under the sound of the Gospel. Members must be faithful to attend the services. Crowds beget crowds. Advertising also brings in people of the city. In a scheduled revival, we are praying that multitudes will come together because of the working of the Lord in our midst.

But the one indispensable prerequisite to revival is **prayer.** Without prayer, the singing, preaching, witnessing, and crowds amount to nothing. We must pray!

Our Lord teaches us the importance of prayer. The Gospels give us some fifteen accounts of Christ praying. He prayed all night. He prayed a great while before day. He prayed in times of crises. He prayed before He raised Lazarus from the dead. He prayed before He went to His own trial and crucifixion. If prayer meant so much in the life of our Saviour, then how much should it mean in our own experience. Surely our powerlessness and failures can be traced to our prayerlessness.

A revival is an event of great importance. Therefore, prayer is an absolute essential to its success.

Now, coming down to the individual, how should we pray?

I. PRAY FOR A WARMING OF HEART

A revival is the reviving of that which has life. Cold hearts are made warm. Indifferent Christians are made concerned.

As we think of revival, we should be praying that our hearts will be warmed by the Spirit of God. Cold hearts are the result of contact with the world. Cold hearts mean we have not stayed close enough to our Saviour. Cold hearts indicate we have allowed an ungodly world to cast a chill upon us.

Doubting hearts are cold hearts. This is illustrated in the story of the two men walking to Emmaus on the resurrection day. When Jesus joined Himself to them, He said, "What manner of communications are these that ye have one to another, as ye walk, and are sad?" When they began to tell Jesus concerning His death and how disappointed they were, He said to them, "O fools, and slow of heart to believe all that the prophets have spoken." He then gave a message concerning Himself. After a time He sat with them at meat in Emmaus. And when their eyes were opened and they knew Him, He vanished out of their sight.

Now we hear them saying, "Did not our heart burn within us while he talked with us by the way, and while he opened to us the scriptures?" (Luke 24:32). Their hearts were made warm by the presence of Christ and by the Word of God from His lips.

As we think of revival, we should pray that God will give us a warming of our hearts, both by His presence and by His Word. May the winter chill be taken away by the warm fervency of His presence. May our doubts be driven away until, like the two people of Emmaus, we will hasten to tell others that we have been with Christ.

II. PRAY FOR A CLEAN HEART

Sincere prayer will always result in facing your sin. If prayer does not bring before your eyes your shortcomings and failures, then you are not praying.

An article in the *Reader's Digest*, written by a Presbyterian minister of Cleveland Heights, Ohio, reminds us of the "calculated risks of prayer." He says the first risk is that of seeing ourselves as we are. We are all prone to excuse ourselves and to dodge knowing ourselves as we are. But prayer invariably causes us to face our own lives and reckon on what we shall do about it.

Second, Dr. Farris says we face the risk of becoming more like Christ. This, too, means the examination of self and a departing from evil.

The third calculated risk is that of having our prayers answered. If we pray for clean hearts, we will have to turn from the sins which have hindered us and caused us to fail.

We need to be definite as we pray for clean hearts. Lack of definiteness is a great hindrance to much of our praying. Sins need to be called by name, whether they be sins known to others or known only to God. Sins of jealousy, malice, hatred and evil speaking need to be confessed. Sins of covetousness and selfishness need to be faced. Sins of evading our responsibility toward God and our fellowman need to be uncovered. Remember, "He that covereth his sins shall not prosper."

Yes, pray for a clean heart; then do something about it!

III. PRAY FOR AN INCREASED LOVE FOR OTHERS

Christ said, "This is my commandment, That ye love one another, as I have loved you" (John 15:12). We have no choice—we must love others. But you answer, "How can we force ourselves to love others?" Perhaps we cannot, but by prayer the Lord will give us hearts that will love our fellow Christians and love the souls of sinful men.

For the Christian, love is the sign that you have passed from death unto life: "We know that we have passed from death unto life, because we love the brethren. He that loveth not his brother abideth in death" (I John 3:14).

In our own midst, at times there have been those who have had the spirit of enmity. They have not loved others. Even members of families have harbored malice in their hearts. Workers in the church have been obsessed by jealousy.

Revivals are hindered by an unforgiving spirit. If revival is to come in our hearts and churches, we must have the spirit of Christ in forgiving others. Holding of grudges will definitely hinder the working of the Holy Spirit.

In my visits to many churches, I soon discover why so few souls are being won and the work is dragging instead of leaping forward. Sometimes it is revealed that there is a feud going on between the deacons or the Sunday school teachers. Sometimes it is the pastor who is not in harmony with the church leaders. He has adopted a very critical attitude, perhaps, because of unfair dealings toward him by his people. Revival fires are quenched when the pastor's heart is not right.

I remember so well conducting a revival in a southern church where it seemed that the situation was hopeless. Souls were not being saved, and Christians were sitting cold and lifeless. The whole situation seemed doomed.

I soon discovered that the pastor and some of his deacons were not in agreement. Bitter feelings were there. I kept on preaching and beseeching Christians to love one another so revival fires might burn.

Finally, on Saturday night, a number of men came forward and knelt at the front. In the group were the offending deacons. When I saw them there, I turned to the pastor and said, "Don't you think you should join them?" He did so. After a time of prayer, the men stood up and with tears began to embrace one another. The differences were gone. The entire atmosphere was changed. And in less than a week, some 250 people were saved.

One pastor came to see me some time ago and told me of a difficulty he was having with his choir director and choir. Finally the spirit became so bitter that the choir director and choir members walked out of the choir and refused to sing again. Some of the people left the church, while others sat in the audience with hard and bitter hearts. Such a spirit hinders revival.

If you are holding a grudge, ask the Lord to help you put it aside. If you need to ask someone to forgive you, then do so without hesitation. If you have been wronged by another, then with a glad heart, forgive.

IV. PRAY FOR A BURDEN FOR SOULS

Some Christians have never had a real burden for souls. When they were saved, they had a temporary desire to see others converted. There was a brief concern for members of their families; then this concern was gone. In such cases, there was never a real burden on their part for the souls of others.

In some cases, you had a burden for souls, but now it is gone. Perhaps for years you were deeply concerned about others, but today you care but little. Make this a matter of prayer. Ask God to give you a burden for souls.

If you haven't a burden, then do the following:

1. *Get a new glimpse of our Saviour dying for you.* See the love of Christ for lost men. See the sacrifice of our Saviour in order that others might be saved.

2. *Read your Bible and get a new vision of the awfulness of eternal Hell.* Think of souls dying and going to Hell and existing there forever and forever. Read the story of Lazarus and Dives. Let the words "torment" and "flames" reach into your consciousness. See the awfulness of an eternal burning Hell.

3. *Pray for sinners by name.* This will help you to have a burden for them. Call their names before God. Pray for their conviction and salvation. Don't be weary in your prayers if the answer does not come quickly. Continue to wait on God until something happens. Be careful

that your prayers do not become mere form. Even praying for others can become a ritual until it is meaningless.

4. *Be ready to witness to others as you have opportunity.* Next to fervent prayer, nothing will burden your heart as definitely talking to the lost. When they refuse your Christ, your heart may be broken. When they accept your Christ, your heart will be made glad. Either way, the burden rests upon you.

Prayer is the one indispensable prerequisite for revival. This is absolutely necessary if our hearts are to be touched and if revival fires are to burn in our midst.

Christians who have been mightily used of God have made prayer a major part of their lives. It was said that Charles Simeon devoted four hours a day to definite prayer. Charles Wesley, the renowned songwriter, gave two hours a day to prayer. John Wesley rose at four o'clock in the morning to pray. John Fletcher sometimes prayed all night. Martin Luther prayed at least three hours a day. John Welch, the mighty Scottish preacher, felt a day was lost if he did not spend eight to ten hours in prayer.

Let us give ourselves to this great ministry of prayer and see what God will do with and through us.

The Sin of Little Praying

"Moreover as for me, God forbid that I should sin against the Lord in ceasing to pray for you: but I will teach you the good and the right way."—I Sam. 12:23.

What an amazing revelation it would be if every Christian walking into this auditorium came bearing a card telling how long each had prayed today (a card written by the hand of God).

One minute? Five minutes? Ten minutes? Or no minutes?

How embarrassed most of us should be at the little amount of time we spend in prayer! Yet I do not want you to think that the worthwhileness of prayer is measured by minutes. Prayer is measured by fervency, honesty and definiteness.

The prayer of Simon Peter, recorded in Matthew 14:30, was not long; but it was certainly fervent and honest. Sinking in the water, Peter cried, "Lord, save me." It was enough!

By "little prayer" I refer to our few prayers and shallow prayers.

Look at the background of our text.

In I Samuel 12:1-5, Samuel proclaimed the kingdom of Israel. In verses 6 to 15, he told of God's deliverances and of their repeated requests for a king. In verses 16 to 25, a miracle was performed. He called down thunder and rain. The people feared and begged for Samuel's help. He promised it to them in verses 23 to 25.

Samuel, the senior—verse 2;

Samuel, the suppliant—verse 23;

Samuel, the serious—verse 24.

I. SAMUEL'S ALIGNMENT WITH GOD

Samuel believed in a God who could speak and call people.

"And the child Samuel ministered unto the Lord before Eli. And the word of the Lord was precious in those days; there was no open vision.

"And it came to pass at that time, when Eli was laid down in his place, and his eyes began to wax dim, that he could not see;

"And ere the lamp of God went out in the temple of the Lord, where the ark of God was, and Samuel was laid down to sleep;

"That the Lord called Samuel: and he answered, Here am I.

"And he ran unto Eli, and said, Here am I; for thou calledst me. And he said, I called not; lie down again. And he went and lay down.

"And the Lord called yet again, Samuel. And Samuel arose and went to Eli, and said, Here am I; for thou didst call me. And he answered, I called not, my son; lie down again.

"Now Samuel did not yet know the Lord, neither was the word of the Lord yet revealed unto him.

"And the Lord called Samuel again the third time. And he arose and went to Eli, and said, Here am I; for thou didst call me. And Eli perceived that the Lord had called the child.

"Therefore Eli said unto Samuel, Go, lie down: and it shall be, if he call thee, that thou shalt say, Speak, Lord; for thy servant heareth. So Samuel went and lay down in his place.

"And the Lord came, and stood, and called as at other times, Samuel, Samuel. Then Samuel answered, Speak; for thy servant heareth."—I Sam. 3:1-10.

He believed in a supernatural God—a God of miracles. Look again at the chapter before us. Read about the thunder and rain in verse 17.

He believed in a God who hates sin. "And Samuel said, Gather all Israel to Mizpeh, and I will pray for you unto the Lord" (I Sam. 7:5).

Samuel's God was altogether different from the god of the modernist. The modernist believes that God allows sin and excuses sin. Not so with Samuel.

Early this morning I heard three people discussing the race problem in Selma, Alabama. They had been in it apparently. Prominent in their discussion was the name of the late Bishop Pike of the Episcopal Church. Pike was a modernist. He denied all.

Not so with Samuel. He was a fundamentalist. He believed in God. He prayed. He knew that God hates sin.

II. SAMUEL'S ACCEPTANCE OF GOD'S VERDICT ON PRAYERLESSNESS

Read I Samuel 12:23 again.

It is a sin against God not to pray. Oh, that this would get home to us!

The sin of little praying for others is because of our selfishness, our forgetfulness and our foolish pride.

We must pray for others or face the fact of our sin.

III. SAMUEL'S AWARENESS OF THE IMPORTANCE OF PRAYER

Our text tells what Samuel thought about prayer.

Prayer brings blessings to others and to you. Peace of heart can only come by prayer. There are blessings through prayer!

Little prayer brings less blessing. Occasional prayer does some good but not as much as faithful praying. No praying robs of all blessings. No praying brings emptiness of life.

We read of the positive declarations in the New Testament on prayer—for example: "And when they had prayed, the place was shaken where they were assembled together; and they were all filled with the Holy Ghost, and they spake the word of God with boldness" (Acts 4:31).

They believed, they prayed, they were filled, and they witnessed.

See the startling vitality of the New Testament church. When we study the attitude and accomplishments of the early church, we see a church of prayer and power!

Dr. Robert Burnette taught his last class on Friday, February 5. Suppose an angel had said to him, "This is your last day to teach. Sunday you will preach in Summerville, Georgia, at the Calvary Baptist Church. But, upon returning home, a car will strike yours. You will be injured, and the injuries will bring you to your death on March 9." I believe that Dr. Burnette would have gone straight on with a gladsome heart, obeying his Saviour.

This is what I want to do!

18 # A Praying Christian

"For my love they are my adversaries: but I give myself unto prayer."—Ps. 109:4.

"But we will give ourselves continually to prayer, and to the ministry of the word."—Acts 6:4.

The right resolutions, made by the impulse of the Holy Spirit, may result in a complete transformation of our lives.

The Word of God will point us to worthwhile endeavors. If a matter is not given in the Bible, we can stay away from it and profit. For example, a man may make a resolution to make money—whatever the price. Does the Word of God approve this? Not at all. The Bible says, "But seek ye first the kingdom of God, and his righteousness; and all these things shall be added unto you" (Matt. 6:33). The Bible says that God "shall supply all your need according to his riches in glory by Christ Jesus" (Phil. 4:19).

Does this mean that the child of God sits down and does nothing? No. The child of God should have a higher endeavor than the seeking of the things of this earth. The Christian who has his attention riveted to eternal values is not concerned primarily about the paltry things of the everyday life.

What does the Bible tell us to do? To trust God, believe the Word, witness to others and pray.

The importance of prayer has been settled for us for all time. We have many illustrations of the power of prayer in individual lives. Therefore, as we think of the new year, we will give time to a brief study of prayer.

I. THE PURPOSE OF PRAYER

Very plainly the Bible says, "Ask, and it shall be given you; seek, and ye shall find; knock, and it shall be opened unto you . . ." (Matt. 7:7).

1. *We are to pray in order to receive things from God.* That we are needy creatures is well established. We can do nothing of ourselves. Since our power is limited, then we must have the help of the Heavenly Father.

It is by prayer that we receive our daily needs. Not only do we obtain things for ourselves, but prayer works on behalf of others.

2. *Prayer is to keep us in fellowship with God.* There must be a contact with our Heavenly Father. By prayer we walk and talk with Him. The man who doesn't pray will have but little to say about God, for his acquaintance will be limited. If I see and converse with a man only once per year, my knowledge of him will be limited. But if I see and talk with him daily, my knowledge will be greater, and I will be much more at home with him.

So it is in the matter of prayer. We must pray in order to know God. We must pray so our fellowship with Him will be real and steadfast.

3. *Prayer will give us peace of heart.* Paul says:

"Be careful for nothing; but in every thing by prayer and supplication with thanksgiving let your requests be made known unto God. And the peace of God, which passeth all understanding, shall keep your hearts and minds through Christ Jesus."—Phil. 4:6, 7.

Billy Sunday once told about a little girl who was obliged to have an operation. Just before receiving the anesthetic, she asked the doctor, "What are you going to do to me?"

The doctor answered, "My dear, we are going to operate; then you will be well again, and run and play as you used to."

"But," the little girl persisted, "what is going to happen now?"

The doctor said, "Darling, we are going to put you to sleep so you won't feel any pain."

Then the child said, "But before going to sleep, I always say my prayers." And in the presence of the physicians, interns and nurses, the little girl climbed down, got on her knees, and said aloud,

> **Now, I lay me down to sleep,**
> **I pray the Lord my soul to keep.**
> **If I should die before I wake,**
> **I pray the Lord my soul to take.**

To this child there came a peace of heart as she committed herself unto the Lord, just as the same prayer must have given to Isaac Watts when he first wrote it and when it was first used in 1732.

It is by prayer that we get things from God, and prayer is how we keep in fellowship with Him and have peace of heart. As we look at our own lives, we can see how much we need the things just mentioned here.

II. THE POWER OF PRAYER

The Bible does not waste time in arguing the effectiveness of prayer, but simply tells us to pray. In I Thessalonians 5:17, Paul said, "Pray without ceasing." Again in verse 25 he said, "Brethren, pray for us." The apostle had no doubt in his mind of the effectiveness and power of prayer.

The Word of God points out conclusively that God answers prayer. For example, in Acts 16 Paul and Silas were praying. As a result of their prayers, there came a great earthquake. Men were loosed from their prison, and Paul and Silas were brought out to preach to the jailer and his household.

God answers prayer. Let no evil influence change your thinking regarding this. Let no person argue and tell you that God doesn't care, doesn't answer. The Word of God proves that He does.

Someone has put down how we should pray.

1. *Pray secretly in the closet of communion:* "But thou, when thou prayest, enter into thy closet, and when thou hast shut thy door, pray to thy Father which is in secret; and thy Father which seeth in secret, shall reward thee openly" (Matt. 6:6).

2. *Pray watchfully, in the alertness of wakefulness:* "Watch and pray, that ye enter not into temptation: the spirit indeed is willing, but the flesh is weak" (Matt. 26:41).

3. *Pray believingly in the simplicity of faith:* "And Jesus answering

saith unto them, Have faith in God" (Mark 11:22).

4. *Pray abidingly in the will of God and in Christ:* "If ye abide in me, and my words abide in you, ye shall ask what ye will, and it shall be done unto you" (John 15:7).

5. *Pray directly in the pointedness of definite petition:* "Elias was a man subject to like passions as we are, and he prayed earnestly that it might not rain: and it rained not on the earth by the space of three years and six months. And he prayed again, and the heaven gave rain, and the earth brought forth her fruit" (James 5:17,18).

6. *Pray effectually in the power of the Spirit:* "But ye, beloved, building up yourselves on your most holy faith, praying in the Holy Ghost" (Jude 20).

All of these words simply tell us that we are to pray and believe in the power of prayer.

Believe that God answers prayer for you as you pray in the name of Jesus and for His will to be done. Your own life can be transformed by the effectiveness of fervent prayer.

Then pray for others. You can easily see changes made in lives because of your effective praying. I am thinking of the story of the Apostle Peter in jail. We are told in Acts 12:5, that the church made prayer without ceasing to God for him. You remember how Peter was released by the angel from the prisonhouse. He came to the meeting place of the Christians and knocked on the door. A damsel came. She recognized Peter's voice and ran in and told the others that Peter stood before the gate. The people said that she was mad, but she affirmed that it was so. Peter stood there still knocking; and when they saw him, they were astonished. But Peter declared how he had been released from prison because of their prayers.

Don't be disturbed when others doubt the effectiveness of prayer, but you continue believing in God and knowing that He never fails to give us what we have need of.

III. THE PLACE OF PRAYER

Child of God, what place should prayer have in your life? Without question or hesitation, most will say, "Prayer should have the first place." In this you are right.

Witnessing is important, but prayer comes first. Prayer makes us ready for witnessing. Prayer creates within us the right spirit and makes us ready to tell others about Christ.

Effective daily living is good, but prayer comes before that. Prayer makes us ready for the tasks of the day.

Church activities must be carried on, but these are best done by those who pray the most.

Nothing is as important as fervent prayer. How long we should pray, where we should pray, how we should pray, will be determined by the individual; but the main thing is to come to God and, in fervent prayer, make your request to Him and believe that God will give an answer.

If we want revival, then there must be much prayer for revival by faithful Christians. The Lord is not going to move in the midst of the great multitudes who profess to know Him unless there is fervent prayer offered. It was prayer that made effective the ministries of Jonathan Edwards, George Whitefield, Charles Finney, D. L. Moody, Reuben Archer Torrey and so many others of God's most-used men.

Daily, earnest, sincere prayer will bring to pass a revival in the nation and in your individual heart.

Someone has said that prayer is the empty hand of need as expressed in the parable of the friend at midnight. Prayer is the cry of despair bringing deliverance. Prayer is the hedge of protection, keeping back the enemy. Prayer is the life's blood coursing through the spiritual being, keeping all in health. Prayer is one weapon which is part of the Christian's armor.

How can we increase our fervency in prayer?

1. *We can study the Word of God until we know what emphasis God places on this matter.* Most people would be greatly shocked if they knew the emphasis given by the Holy Spirit to fervent prayer.

2. *We can be ashamed of ourselves for our prayerlessness.* It was J. H. Jowett who said, "I am so often ashamed of my prayers. They so frequently cost me nothing. They shed no blood. I am amazed at the grace and condescension of my Lord, that He confers any fruitfulness upon my superficial pains."

Let us be ashamed that we pray so little and so carelessly.

3. *We can endeavor to let our hearts be touched by the need to pray.* Too often we think we can work out all our difficulties by ourselves. Therefore, we fail to take our needs to the Lord in prayer. May God touch our hearts and give us a yearning to pray.

4. *We can give ourselves to earnest prayer.* Remember, all mighty men of the Bible were men of prayer, and all men and women greatly used throughout the world have spent much time in prayer.

There is no greater power in the world than prayer. True prayer can do anything when directed by the Holy Spirit and presented to God in the name of Jesus Christ. Prayer is work. It involves an utmost expenditure of the heart's vitality.

The coming year can be one of blessing for you, if you determine now to give yourself to prayer. More than blessing, it can be a year of real accomplishment for our blessed Lord.

19 | Altar-Builders

"And Noah builded an altar unto the Lord."—Gen. 8:20.

"And the Lord appeared unto Abram, and said, Unto thy seed will I give this land: and there builded he an altar unto the Lord, who appeared unto him."—Gen. 12:7.

Abraham was a mighty man of prayer. He built his altars to God, and God talked with him. He was an altar-builder, so consequently his life was altar-blessed. Before Abraham's time, another man builded an altar. It is written, "But Noah found grace in the eyes of the Lord" (Gen. 6:8).

We have been so busy building houses, cities and nations that we have left off building altars. We have come a long way from the simple living of Abraham's day. The centuries have widened the chasm between God and man. God is still the same: but man, by occupation and preoccupation, has drawn a curtain between himself and God. That curtain is woven of an earthy fabric. It is made up of the sinful, shameful, neglectful, godless conduct of man. Only now and then does some person pierce that curtain and talk to God and learn the true meaning of prayer.

Many lessons are to be derived from the altar building of Noah and Abraham. Let us see a few of them.

I. WE NEED A PLACE OF PRAYER

Each of us needs a place where we can go aside and talk to God, a place apart from others, a place where we can pour out our hearts, telling God all of our difficulties and heartaches.

And then there needs to be a place and time for family prayer—a family altar. Because of the congested time schedule and the congested living conditions in many homes, all of this is hard. But the greater the effort, the greater the blessings.

Choose the time best suited for all family members and make an altar unto God. Let this be a time when God's Word is read—if only a few verses—and each member of the family offers up a fervent prayer to the Lord.

II. WHEN BEGINNING A NEW PHASE IN LIFE—PRAY!

When the floodwaters abated and Noah and those who were saved in the ark began a new life upon a cleansed earth, "Noah builded an altar unto the Lord." Then the Lord gave His promise and blessing to Noah.

When Abraham by faith left Haran and entered the land of Canaan, the first thing he did was to build an altar and call upon the name of the Lord. Read Genesis 12:7,8:

"And the Lord appeared unto Abram, and said, Unto thy seed will I give this land: and there builded he an altar unto the Lord, who appeared unto him. And he removed from thence unto a mountain on the east of Bethel, and pitched his tent, having Bethel on the west, and Hai on the east: and there he builded an altar unto the Lord, and called upon the name of the Lord."

What an example for us! When beginning any new phase of life, pray!

1. *Young people, when you are ready to launch out into your life's work, pray for God's guidance and blessing.* Pray to make sure that you are doing what God wants you to do. Prayer will save you from needless regrets later on.

One of the unhappiest men I have ever met was a clerk in a feed store in Louisville, Kentucky, a man past fifty years of age. He said, "My life has been one long misfit. God called me to special service when I was young, and now for thirty years I have lived in the consciousness that I was not doing what God wanted me to do."

2. *When you are beginning a new business, ask God to bless and help.* Not many men do this. They figure out everything and check it again and again. They fail to take God into partnership with them. It is no mere chance that some men have succeeded greatly in life. Mr. R. G. LeTourneau opened every one of his great plants after much prayer, and every plant started off with a revival meeting. A businessman in Georgia arranged for Evangelist Roy Austin to speak to his employees every day for two weeks. They took the time off and sat down to hear the Gospel. It cost the businessman hundreds of dollars, but, oh, the blessing he and the others received!

3. *When beginning a home, or building a home, pray.* I have been invited only a few times in my life to read God's Word and pray in a newly built home. I wish I could have this experience many times.

III. AFTER YOUR MISTAKES, PRAY!

After the almost tragic mistake of Abraham down in Egypt, when he had lied about his wife, he went back to Bethel and there called on the name of the Lord (Gen. 13:4).

After your mistakes, after your failures, after your moments of spiritual weakness, go back to Bethel. Search out at once a place of prayer and tell God about it. What would we do if we could not pray about our mistakes? What would we do if God did not tear up the old spoiled pages and give us a new clean sheet to write upon?

Thanks be unto God for His wonderful provision for the sons of men. He knows our weakness. He knows we are going to make mistakes. He knows that sin will creep in unawares.

If your life is wrong, tell God all about it and ask His forgiveness. Tell Him how mean you have been. Don't hold back a thing. A lot of Christians are weak and sickly because they did wrong and stayed wrong. Get back to Bethel. Sin will try to keep you from the place of prayer. "Prayer will keep you from sin, or sin will keep you from the place of prayer."

Psalm 51, a prayer wrung from the heart of David, has three cries: (1) a cry of confession: "I acknowledge my transgressions"; (2) a cry for cleansing: "Purge me with hyssop, and I shall be clean: wash me, and I shall be whiter than snow"; (3) a cry for consecration: "Then will I teach transgressors thy ways; and sinners shall be converted unto thee." Noah, an altar-builder, confessed his mistakes to God.

Abraham, an altar-builder, was a man of imperfections who, after his mistakes, prayed.

IV. WHEN DEALING WITH OTHERS, PRAY!

This means that you will have to pray all the time, unless you find a desert island and live the life of a hermit.

Prayer gave Abraham a right attitude toward others, and especially toward a worldly, selfish, trouble-making nephew named Lot. To deal with this troublesome world, you need to be a praying Christian.

1. *In business, your fellowman will exhibit untold potentialities for selfishness.* Only much prayer can give you the Spirit of Christ.

Abraham and Lot came to the parting of their ways, recorded in Genesis 13. When big-hearted Abraham said, "Take your choice," and Lot took the best of the land, the old altar-builder was untroubled.

2. *In social life, your friends may snub you, but prayer will give you a right attitude.* Personally, this doesn't bother me, but it does bother some people. It bothers young people when they are ignored and snubbed by others. When you take it to the Lord in prayer, He will show you that it doesn't matter. He will keep your heart right.

3. *In religious matters, we must pray much.* The soul winner suffers many rebuffs. You will be insulted at times. A door slammed in your face will be your only thanks for trying to show your interest in the spiritual welfare of another. But remember, keep on praying. They slammed the doors on Jesus. He was a social outcast. The so-called best people would not allow Him inside their homes. Yes, and they crucified Him, too!

There is only one reason why I continue to preach and try to win souls—JESUS. There is only one reason why I willingly take the indifference and sneers of men—JESUS.

They spat on Him, slapped His face, pressed a crown of thorns upon His brow. They jeered at Him who is King of kings, drove cruel nails in His hands and feet. Yet He could pray, "Father, forgive them, for they know not what they do."

If Jesus could do that, then can't we keep on praying and working for Him?

When dealing with others, pray. Especially pray when dealing with those out of Christ. There may be many long, discouraging times when answers are slow; but God will answer if you pray in faith, believing.

Dr. A. T. Pierson went to hear George Mueller speak on prayer and the way God had answered his prayers through the years. After it was over, he went to Mr. Mueller and asked if he had ever petitioned God for anything that had not been granted.

"Sixty-two years, three months, five days and two hours have passed," replied Mr. Mueller, with his characteristic exactness, "since I began to pray for two men to be converted. I have prayed daily for them ever since, and as yet, neither shows any signs of turning to God."

"Do you expect God to convert them?"

"Certainly," was the confident reply. "Do you think that God would lay on His child such a burden for over sixty years if He had no purpose for their conversion?"

Both men were saved a short time after the death of Mr. Mueller.

God answers prayer!

Taught by the Spirit

"Likewise the Spirit also helpeth our infirmities: for we know not what we should pray for as we ought: but the Spirit itself [Himself] *maketh intercession for us with groanings which cannot be uttered. And he that searcheth the hearts knoweth what is the mind of the Spirit, because he maketh intercession for the saints according to the will of God."*—Rom. 8:26,27.

(Read all verses in Romans 8 referring to the Holy Spirit and His work.)

What is prayer?

Prayer is the soul conversing with God. Prayer is God's appointed way for communion between Him and man. Someone said, "Prayer is the crying of an infant in the night." The definition has value; but it is not perfect, for sometimes the infant is ignored. I don't believe God ever ignores the cries of His children.

Prayer is putting ourselves into God's hands. Prayer is offering God our petitions for mercies needed and our thanks for mercies obtained. Prayer embraces invocation, supplication, intercession, thanksgiving. Prayer is God's way for His children to obtain what they need.

Prayer is not easy. The world, the flesh and the Devil war against us when we pray. The praying Christian finds discouragement from the world. The flesh is not interested in prayer. And there comes a strange, evil work against you, which originates from the Devil, to try to keep you from praying. You feel your need of prayer; you want to pray; still the opposition is there.

Please note: Without prayer we cannot be victorious. Without prayer we cannot achieve in the spiritual realm for God. Prayer has been a part of every outstanding life.

Yes, we will have opposition; but, thank God, we have the Holy Spirit to help us.

From Romans 8 I want us to see the message on prayer and the aid given us by the Spirit of God.

I. THE HELPING SPIRIT

"Likewise the Spirit also helpeth our infirmities...."—Rom. 8:26.

We are weak. We blunder. We make innumerable mistakes. But our troubles are but a small part of the trouble engulfing the entire world. "For we know that the whole creation groaneth and travaileth in pain together until now" (Rom. 8:22).

Because of the constant troubles on every hand, we must depend upon the Holy Spirit to help us as we come to pray.

1. *The Holy Spirit helps our understanding.*

"Howbeit when he, the Spirit of truth, is come, he will guide you into all truth: for he shall not speak of himself; but whatsoever he shall hear, that shall he speak: and he will shew you things to come."— John 16:13.

The Holy Spirit helps us understand the Bible. Keep in mind that this is the Spirit-inspired Word; and, therefore, the best Interpreter for us is the Spirit of God.

This letter came to me from a gentleman in Illinois:

Dear Brother Roberson:

In this area there are several ministers that came through your school, and I question some of the doctrines they teach. And did you teach these things at your school, such as Immortality of the Soul, The Rapture, Hell Fire, Jesus is God? These sorts of things cause a lot of confusion and babbling. What about these things?

Yours truly,
(Name withheld)

P.S. Julius T. Lyons told me I wouldn't live long, and that I would burn in Hell, for being a dedicated servant of Jehovah. Can you make such a narrow statement?

This man sent along a tract entitled, *What Do Jehovah's Witnesses Believe?*

I had an answer for this friend. We do teach the immortality of the soul, the rapture, Hell-fire, Jesus is God; and what Julius T. Lyons said is true: unless this man repents of his sin and believes in Jesus Christ, the Son of God, he will burn in Hell.

All of the heresies of this day come, not because of the Holy Spirit's leading and teaching, but because of man's ideas. The Holy Spirit will help us understand God's Holy Word and help us know our place in this present world.

2. *The Holy Spirit helps us bear our burdens.* Some burdens we must bear, such as concern for souls. This burden we should have all of our lifetime. We cannot bear this burden without the aid of the blessed Holy Spirit.

Again, there are some sorrows that are always with us. We must not try to bear these heartaches alone, but depend on the Holy Spirit, given to comfort and help us.

"Nevertheless I tell you the truth; It is expedient for you that I go away: for if I go not away, the Comforter will not come unto you; but if I depart, I will send him unto you."—John 16:7.

3. *The Holy Spirit lifts our burdens.* Yes, some burdens we must bear, but there are some that He will lift from our hearts. He will help us to find our place in this present age. He will teach us about the things of this world. The Holy Spirit will free our hearts from being burdened about material things if we will simply let Him drive into our consciousness the Word of God.

"But seek ye first the kingdom of God, and his righteousness; and all these things shall be added unto you. Take therefore no thought for the morrow: for the morrow shall take thought for the things of itself. Sufficient unto the day is the evil thereof."—Matt. 6:33, 34.

Some are burdened about certain situations that they cannot help. The position in which you find yourself is not of your making. God doesn't intend you to be burdened about it, and the Holy Spirit will lift that burden if you will let Him.

4. *The Holy Spirit convicts of sin.* Sin hinders prayer. This Bible says, "If I regard iniquity in my heart, the Lord will not hear me" (Ps. 66:18). If we are to get through to God, then the Holy Spirit has to work in our hearts, convicting and showing us what to do and what not to do. If He is grieved, then we cannot have freedom in prayer. Paul tells us, "And grieve not the holy Spirit of God whereby ye are sealed unto the day of redemption" (Eph. 4:30). The apostle tells us to put away bitterness, wrath, anger, clamor, evil speaking, and all malice, and be kind one to another.

The indwelling Holy Spirit will help us to pray. We sinners, saved by grace, desperately need His help.

II. THE INTERCEDING SPIRIT

"*. . . The Spirit itself* [Himself] *maketh intercession for us with groanings which cannot be uttered. And he that searcheth the hearts knoweth what is the mind of the Spirit, because he maketh intercession for the saints according to the will of God.*"—Rom. 8:26, 27.

The Holy Spirit indwells us. He intercedes for us. On occasions we are overcome by the burdens of life. Our prayers may be no more than a simple groaning to God; but the Bible tells us, 'The Spirit maketh intercession for us with groanings which cannot be uttered.'

It is interesting to notice how Paul uses the word "groan" twice in this chapter. He speaks of the earth—"For we know that the whole creation groaneth and travaileth in pain together until now." Then he speaks also of the Holy Spirit 'making intercession for us with groanings which cannot be uttered.'

In the dark hours, when prayer is hard and the way seems impossible, He intercedes for us.

Christian friend, remember that you are not alone. The Holy Spirit is with you, and 'He makes interession for you.'

"We must remember that we, too, must be intercessors. This means that we must pray for others.

We will never know until we stand in the presence of the Lord, the impact of intercessors. What miracles have taken place because of prayers of others—for preachers, for missionaries, for children, for parents, for teachers, for loved ones.

Intercessory prayer is good for us all. Praying for others will keep your interest high in the spiritual welfare for others. Praying for others will create a love for those we scarcely know. We may be earnestly praying for someone that we have never seen. Praying for others will help us to be interested in the work that others are doing.

A pastor was conducting a funeral service for a man of his church. After the service, the wife of the departed one told the pastor that in thirty years of married life, she did not remember one morning ever having passed without having family worship. Then she said that in thirty years she had never heard her husband close his season of prayer without saying this, "Lord, help us to make somebody happy today."

It should be the joy of our hearts to pray for others and thereby to see good things happen to them because of our fervent prayers. We should endeavor, by our prayer life, to bring joy and blessing to many around us.

There is an old legend that has been told of an aged believer. They say that he lived in a cave near a swift-flowing river. It was his duty to take upon his shoulders and bear across whoever wished to gain the opposite shore. Many a tired traveler he bore across the flood, manfully buffeting the billows.

One night, weary from the day's toil, he fell asleep. The weather was cold, dark and stormy. The river's current was raging fiercely. Above the roar of the torrent and the screech of the winds, he heard a cry. Springing from his couch, he plunged into the wild night. Taking his pole, he waded across the swollen rapid. As he reached the other side, he saw a child of wondrous beauty waiting to be carried to the other side.

Taking him upon his shoulders, he started to cross. Just as they were stepping into the dangerous channel in the center of the raging flood, the child's sweet voice said, "When thou passest through the waters, I will be with thee." Then the old hermit knew that it was the child Jesus whom he carried. His arms then became strong, and his heart light and glad.

Only a legend, but it has some truth in it for all of us. We need to pray for others, to be concerned about people that blessings might come to their hearts and that they might be brought near to the Saviour because of the fervency of our prayers and our concern for them.

III. THE LEADING SPIRIT

"For as many as are led by the Spirit of God, they are the sons of God."—Rom. 8:14.

"There is therefore now no condemnation to them which are in Christ Jesus, who walk not after the flesh, but after the Spirit."—Rom. 8:1.

"That the righteousness of the law might be fulfilled in us, who walk not after the flesh, but after the Spirit."—Rom. 8:4.

The children of God manifest to the world that they are redeemed as they are led by the Holy Spirit. He leads us in Bible study, in prayer, in Christian service. He leads us in worship and in all endeavors of the church.

The leading Spirit! This brings to us the matter of the fullness of the Spirit as He possesses us. He illumines our mind, quickens our consciousness, and teaches us what to pray for.

Therefore, we should hunger for the fullness of the Spirit; for when we are filled with the Spirit, we will pray as God directs.

1. *He leads us in making decisions.* How true this was in the ministry of the Apostle Paul! The Holy Spirit forbade him to go into a certain area and preach the Gospel, but He led him into another situation. So it will be in your life and mine. Wait for the Holy Spirit to guide in making your decisions. Don't be swayed by friends and families; don't be sidetracked by the alluring offers of the world— but be led by the Holy Spirit.

2. *He leads us in doing what God has prescribed for us.* Every Christian has a job to do. In the doing of that task, He gives His guidance.

3. *He leads us in helping others to know Christ.* The constant aim of every Christian should be to win souls. This is done only under the leadership of the Holy Spirit.

The Man Whose Prayers Failed

". . . but Abraham stood yet before the Lord."—Gen. 18:22.

"And the Lord went his way, as soon as he had left communing with Abraham: and Abraham returned unto his place."—Gen. 18:33.

"Then the Lord rained upon Sodom and upon Gomorrah brimstone and fire from the Lord out of heaven; And he overthrew those cities, and all the plain, and all the inhabitants of the cities, and that which grew upon the ground."—Gen. 19:24,25.

". . . But Abraham stood yet before the Lord"—few words in Scripture are as beautiful. The friend of God, the father of the faithful, stood before the Lord. Abraham, perhaps the most influential man in the Old Testament, was a man of prayer.

He stood before the Lord to pray for a city where sin was rampant, and where Satan was king. 'The sin of Sodom and Gomorrah was grievous.'

He prayed, but the city was destroyed. His prayers for Sodom failed, but Abraham's failure to save Sodom in no way lessens his eminence in Christian thinking.

Now, consider three thoughts:

I. ABRAHAM, THE FRIEND OF GOD

When Abraham was called out by the Lord, he received the promise from God that he would be a blessing. In a very definite way the hand of God was upon this man.

"Now the Lord had said unto Abram, Get thee out of thy country, and from thy kindred, and from thy father's house, unto a land that I will shew thee:

"And I will make of thee a great nation, and I will bless thee, and make thy name great; and thou shalt be a blessing:

"And I will bless them that bless thee, and curse him that curseth thee: and in thee shall all families of the earth be blessed."—Gen. 12:1-3.

Abraham was not perfect, but he always returned to the Lord, and God renewed His promise toward him. The outstanding thing about Abraham was his prayer life. He stayed at the altar of God.

1. *He prayed earnestly.* In the story before us, his earnestness is evident. Love made him concerned about Lot and Sodom. His compassion of heart made him care for others.

There is but one way to pray, and that is in earnest. How childish and infantile are many prayers of this day when they are read from books and recited without thought. To get something from God, there must be compassion and meaning, an earnestness.

2. *He prayed patiently.* Read the story as given in Genesis 18. He first asked the Lord if He would spare the city if fifty righteous were found within it. God said He would spare the place if fifty were found. Then Abraham asked God to spare the city if forty-five could be found. God responded that He would save it for forty-five. Then Abraham came to forty, thirty, twenty, then down to ten. Perhaps Abraham thought there were surely ten in the city, but there were not. His prayer for the city failed, but Abraham's prayer for Lot's family was heard.

We are living in a world of great sin and corruptness. People are confused. The leaders of nations are at their wit's end. The shadows of war are constantly around us. The tragedy is that so many people seem to care nothing for the things of Christ. They are lost, bound by the sin of the world, and ripe for destruction.

Are we praying patiently for them to be saved? Are we beseeching God for our friends, neighbors and loved ones to come to Jesus Christ?

3. *He prayed believingly.* Abraham believed in God. He knew that

God was with him. He knew where he stood before the Lord. He offered his prayers believing that God would do for him that which was best.

Someone has said that prayer and the promises are interdependent.

> The promise inspires and energizes prayer. But prayer locates the promise and gives it realization and location. The promise is like the blessed rain falling in full showers; but prayer like the pipes which transmit, preserve, and direct the rain, localizes and precipitates these promises until they become local and personal and bless, refresh, and fertilize.

Pray believingly, knowing that God hears and answers prayer. Pray submissively, knowing that by our submission we gain access to the presence of God.

4. *His prayer brought blessing to Lot, though it failed to save Sodom.* We must pray for others. Sometimes the answer may not be exactly as we desire, but it will be what God desires for us.

The greatest of blessings will come to people when we pray in their behalf. God's great men have always prayed; yea, they were great because they did pray.

Pray for others! Keep a prayer list with the names of all who are heavy upon your heart, and pray for them daily.

I was reading this week of a woman who was in a home for incurables. She was paralyzed so completely that she couldn't move even a finger. She couldn't brush away a hair or a fly from her face, let alone feed herself.

That woman was a mighty prayer warrior. She had a prayer list of several hundred pastors, evangelists, missionaries and others in God's service. When she prayed for them, she was laying up for herself treasures in Heaven. What a reward she will have when she stands before the Lord Jesus and knows the fullness of all of her prayers for others!

Is there someone praying for you? Then thank God, rejoice and move forward. Are you praying for others? I trust you are. Prayer brings us into the circle of the eternal.

II. LOT, A CHRISTIAN OUT OF PLACE

When we study the life of Lot, we see a similarity to many people of our day and time. Lot was an uncertain individual and out of the will of God. His best recommendation was his relationship to Abraham.

1. *Lot sought the big place.* This has often spelled destruction. When you seek the big place, the world, the flesh and the Devil are your allies. Lot sought the place of eminence and lost everything. He wanted to be rich, wanted to be a ruler of others; but he came down to nothing and lost all that he had.

In recent months two ministers of my acquaintance left the ministry after years of service. Both were preachers of ability, but they left the ministry to take positions that would bring them some returns of the world. Such men are following after Lot. They are seeking the big place and will suffer. Chastisement will be upon them. They will lose peace and joy. Don't follow after Lot. Don't seek for the big place in life.

2. *Lot was miserable, for he was out of the place God had for him.* He associated with evil men and had no influence with his own family. They laughed at him, mocked him. Though recognized in the Scriptures as a man of God, there was little about him that would recommend him to sacred company.

Let your heart go out in sorrow for the man who is out of God's place for him. Let your sympathy go to him. Remember, he is miserable and useless. He is like Simon Peter following Jesus afar off. He is like John Mark leaving the company of Barnabas and Saul. He is like Demas who forsook the apostle and returned to Thessalonica.

God has a definite place for you. Fill that place. Obey God, and His blessings will be upon you. If you run from that place and seek the things of this world, misery, unhappiness and loss will be yours.

3. *Lot was delivered from Sodom, but only because of the grace of God.* Abraham prayed for a city, but got only Lot and his family. He was delivered from Sodom, but the rest of the story gives little of beauty and usefulness. And yet, we are happy that the Word of

God speaks of "just Lot" (II Pet. 2:7,8).

O friend, obey God! Don't be foolish and waste God-given time. Do what God says—and do it now. What a sad story is this one! What a poor testimony! Lot knew better, but he went astray, even as you may go astray if you follow the flesh.

III. SODOM, THE CITY OF SIN

"And the Lord said, Because the cry of Sodom and Gomorrah is great, and because their sin is very grievous. . . ."—Gen. 18:20.

What was it that destroyed Sodom? Sin. The city was destroyed though Abraham had prayed for it. The judgment of God fell, for God must judge sin.

A truth that we must recognize is the judgment of sin. If we fail in judging sin, then God will judge it. Sodom fell because of Sodom's sin. Sodom refused to turn to God, and there was nothing else that a sinless God could do but destroy that wicked place. Now, remember two things:

1. *Chastening must come upon the Christian for his sin.* Lot suffered because of his evil. Abraham also suffered when he did what was wrong. When you do wrong, chastening is coming. If you persist in wrong, death may come to take you. Let us read again from Hebrews 12:5,6:

"My son, despise not thou the chastening of the Lord, nor faint when thou art rebuked of him: For whom the Lord loveth he chasteneth, and scourgeth every son whom he receiveth."

2. *Judgment must come upon this evil world.* Let no man think he can escape the judgment of God. Face now with solemnity the fact that one day you must stand before God and be judged. The matter of judgment has been settled in the Book of God.

A young minister was confronted by an able young skeptic. At the close of the service the skeptic came to the preacher and said, "You did well, but you know I do not believe in the infallibility of the Bible."

The young preacher made one simple, calm assertion: "It is appointed unto men once to die, but after this the judgment."

The skeptic said, "I can prove to you that there is no such thing as the judgment after death."

The young preacher answered, "But men do die, 'For it is appointed unto men once to die, but after this the judgment.' "

The skeptic said, "But that's no argument. Let's get down to business and discuss this matter in regular form."

The pastor said, "I am here to preach the Word of God, not to argue over it."

The skeptic, annoyed, turned away with this remark, "I don't believe you know enough about the Bible to argue about it."

The preacher replied calmly, "Perhaps you are right, but remember this: 'It is appointed unto men once to die, but after this the judgment.' "

The skeptic went away and seemed to hear only one thing—"judgment, judgment, judgment."

The next morning he made a call at the parsonage. He said, "I have come to see you about that verse of Scripture you gave me last night. I have spent a terrible night with those words burning their way into my soul. I can't get rid of them. Tell me what I must do to be saved. I've got to get rid of this torture!"

When he left, he was a child of God through faith in the finished work of Christ.

Sinner friend, see and know that you must one day come to judgment. The day of the great white throne is just ahead for you. At that time you will stand before the Saviour, the One you rejected, and be judged for your works. You will stand there as a lost sinner, and the judgment will determine the extent of your punishment in the place called Hell.

3. *The only place of safety is in Jesus Christ.* The door of salvation is open. Will you receive Him as Saviour? Judgment is coming. Without Christ you are unprepared.

In London, England, there used to stand a somber, heavy stone building called Newgate Prison. We are told that the last execution that took place in that prison was of a poor woman who had been sentenced to death for an awful deed.

Her last night was spent in the cell allotted to those who have been condemned to die. Early the next morning at seven o'clock she was to suffer.

About six o'clock when the jailers went into the cell, they found her quietly sleeping and smiling as she lay so near death. They didn't have the heart to awaken her, so they left her for another half hour.

Again they came, but still she slept. They noticed the peaceful smile upon her face. They learned afterwards that she was dreaming of the early days of her childhood when she lived in the village home, peacefully and happily. She was dreaming of her father and mother, her brothers and sisters, of innocent days in the fields gathering flowers, roaming the quiet lanes in the still evenings of summer days.

The jailers wept as they saw the sight of the woman with the smile upon her face, but yet they had to awaken her. Awaken her they did. As she came back to consciousness and remembered where she was and that which was going to happen, she gave a bitter, piercing scream, never to be forgotten by those who heard it.

There is one day an awakening for every sinner. At this time the reality of condemnation, judgment and eternity will be seen and realized. What a drastic and tragic hour it will be when men see their lost condition! They will call for the mountains to fall upon them and to cover them from the wrath of the Lamb.

I repeat: there is but one safe place, and that is in Jesus Christ. Will you receive Him as your Saviour now?

"Verily, verily, I say unto you, He that heareth my word, and believeth on him that sent me, hath everlasting life, and shall not come into condemnation; but is passed from death unto life."—John 5:24.

The Power of Prayer

"The sacrifice of the wicked is an abomination to the Lord: but the prayer of the upright is his delight."—Prov. 15:8.

"Be careful for nothing; but in every thing by prayer and supplication with thanksgiving let your requests be made known unto God. And the peace of God, which passeth all understanding, shall keep your hearts and minds through Christ Jesus."—Phil. 4:6,7.

Christians need help!

David said, "The righteous cry, and the Lord heareth, and delivereth them out of all their troubles" (Ps. 34:17).

I need God's help every day, His wisdom, His strength. Christians need help in facing and conquering the temptations of life. Satan is ever busy putting temptations before us.

Christians need help in overcoming the weaknesses of the flesh. There is no man without human weakness. Christians need help in handling the thorny situations of life. We face problems beyond our wisdom to handle! I have them.

Christians need help in meeting and conquering the enemies of God and the cross.

All you need, He will supply. Remember, you are His child. Remember, He has promised to supply your needs. He cannot break His promise. His promises have been given!

Joshua prayed and God answered. David prayed and God answered. Jonah prayed, Daniel prayed, the disciples prayed, Paul prayed, and God answered!

One question comes to mind: Why don't men pray?

1. *They do not believe.* The unsaved person does not believe. He cannot pray. The doubting person does not believe. He doubts the promises of God. Even good Christians sometimes doubt.

2. *Man is impatient.* He thinks God is too slow. He takes things in his own hands. But we need to be patient, pray and wait! WAIT! I have seen answers to prayers days, months, and even years after they were offered. David admonishes, "Rest in the Lord, and *wait* patiently for him" (Ps. 37:7).

3. *Men are ignorant and blind to the promises of God.* There are 32,000 promises in the Bible. They are yours, they are mine! Great Christians believe the promises. One promise Jesus made was, "I will never leave thee, nor forsake thee."

4. *Man is ungrateful (and forgetful)!* God answers prayers, but we don't thank Him. We go on our way—ungrateful. Ingratitude will sever the prayer line. Remember His blessings; then express your gratitude.

5. *Men don't pray because of pride.* Oh, the proud hearts of men! "Pride goeth before destruction, and an haughty spirit before a fall," says Proverbs 16:18.

All believers should pray, and say that they do! The President, the king, the millionaire, the pauper—all should pray and believe God! Prime Minister Gladstone was one who prayed.

Christian friend, prayer will change you!

"But they that wait upon the Lord shall renew their strength; they shall mount up with wings as eagles; they shall run, and not be weary; and they shall walk, and not faint."—Isa. 40:31.

We need submission to God. We need flexibility, to follow Him. Prayer will change you!

Prayer will also change others. Go on, pray for that loved one! God can change them. He can change the haughty, the mean, the brutal. He can change the attitude of the lost.

Prayer will change situations. When Elijah prayed on Mount Carmel, the situation changed. When the disciples prayed for Peter in jail, the situation changed (Acts 12).

Homes, businesses, nations can be changed.

"If my people, which are called by my name, shall humble themselves, and pray, and seek my face, and turn from their wicked ways; then will I hear from heaven, and will forgive their sin, and will heal their land."—II Chron. 7:14.

What is prayer?

I. PRAYER IS OUR TOUCH WITH GOD

Every believer can live in touch with God. How? By prayer. What a thought!!

Moses lived in touch with God. God directed Moses—remember the burning bush experience. God strengthened Moses when he was sometimes weak (Exod. 32).

Joshua lived in touch with God through prayer. Read the story of Achan in Joshua 7.

Samuel lived in touch with God through prayer. ". . . God forbid that I should sin against the Lord in ceasing to pray for you" (I Sam. 12:23).

David lived in touch with God through prayer. Read the Psalms. Then in Psalm 51 we hear David's cry for forgiveness.

Jeremiah lived in touch with God through prayer. He was called the weeping prophet.

Daniel lived in touch with God through prayer. Three times per day he prayed with his windows open toward Jerusalem. He feared not, for God was with him.

Our Lord Jesus lived in touch with God: "And in the morning, rising up a great while before day, he went out, and departed into a solitary place, and there prayed" (Mark 1:35).

Read of Jesus praying in the Garden of Gethsemane in Luke 22:39-46.

How dare any of us try to live without prayer! We are weak, limited, ignorant, so we must pray!

II. PRAYER IS THE DOOR TO GOD'S STOREHOUSE OF BLESSING

"Ask, and it shall be given you; seek, and ye shall find; knock, and

it shall be opened unto you: For every one that asketh receiveth; and he that seeketh findeth; and to him that knocketh it shall be opened."—Matt. 7:7,8.

". . . yet ye have not, because ye ask not."—James 4:2.

Here is God's promise: "But my God shall supply all your need according to his riches in glory by Christ Jesus" (Phil. 4:19). He will supply your needs!

Evangelist Lester Roloff believed that. He prayed and God answered. George Mueller believed that. He prayed and God answered. He cared for thousands of children.

Camp Joy is a work of prayer. Tennessee Temple University is a work of prayer. We prayed and God answered!

We fail in our faith. Believe the promises of God. We fail in our fervency. Be "fervent in spirit." We fail in faithfulness. Keep at it—in season and out of season.

III. PRAYER IS THE WAY TO VICTORIOUS LIVING

There can be no victory in life without prayer. There can be no Christlikeness without prayer. Christ was a man of prayer. Christlikeness means separation from the world, so we can pray! There can be no fullness of the Spirit without prayer. Ephesians 5:18 bids us, ". . . be filled with the Spirit." The early Christians were filled and empowered.

Prayer is essential! The position while praying can vary—kneeling, Dr. John Rice (in Monroe, Louisiana); sitting, while driving his car—Dr. Ernest I. Reveal; walking—Dr. Oswald J. Smith.

There can be no solutions to life's problems without prayer. What is your problem? God has the answer. Not *an* answer, but *the* answer—the right answer.

There can be no peace without prayer. Read again Philippians 4:6 and 7. Oh, this troubled world is without peace. We are so unsettled, nervous, sinful. Thousands commit suicide yearly. The mental institutions are filled. The psychiatrists and psychologists are kept busy. Pray, believe and have peace!

IV. PRAYER IS ESSENTIAL IN THE GREATEST WORK—WINNING THE LOST

Do you pray for others? In my meetings, I ask people to raise their hands if they are concerned about praying for loved ones. Some give me names of loved ones to pray for. I have seen answers to prayers recently in Jacksonville, Florida, and in other places. In Springfield, Tennessee, there were 111 requests for prayer for loved ones. Prayer moves hearts. I asked Dr. E. R. Wadsworth once to pray for me. Some years later when I saw him, I asked him if he had been praying for me. He immediately flipped through a book and pointed to number 473. There was my name, and he said he had prayed for me every day since he told me he would. I was impressed and humbled.

Pray for yourself, that God will use you. Pray for power! Pray for the fullness of the Spirit. And be sure to meet God's requirements as you pray.

Pray for all of the services in God's house.

Oh, the power of prayer!

The Man Who Prayed to Die

"Yet now, if thou wilt forgive their sin—; and if not, blot me, I pray thee, out of thy book which thou hast written."—Exod. 32:32.

Exodus 32 is filled with headline stories. For example: "People Worship Golden Calf," "Three Thousand Slain in Israel's Camp," "Moses, Leader of Israel, Grieved by Evil."

Moses was on Mount Sinai when gross mischief took place among the children of Israel. When Moses delayed returning, they appealed to Aaron, the brother of Moses, to make them gods.

Aaron, a very accommodating religious leader (a type of the compromising, convictionless leaders of many major denominations), told the people to bring their gold. They did so, and he fashioned the gold into a molten calf and said, "These be thy gods, O Israel, which brought thee up out of the land of Egypt."

Look at the introduction to this story.

1. *The cry of the people.* They cried, "Make us gods!" I am amazed that these, who had been led by the Lord for so many days, could now come to the place where they would forsake the one true God and ask that gods be made for them.

Here we have evidence that the best of people can fall into the worst of sins.

2. *The condemnation of Jehovah.* God spoke to Moses and told him to get down from the mount because the people had corrupted themselves. Then the Lord said, "Moses, I have seen this people, and,

behold, it is a stiffnecked people: Now therefore let me alone, that my wrath may wax hot against them, and that I may consume them: and I will make of thee a great nation."

It was in the heart of God to destroy the people of Israel because of their tragic sin. Only the prayer of Moses stayed the hand of God.

3. *The crucible of righteous anger.* When Moses came down from the mount, he carried with him the two tables of the law. When Moses came down to the camp and saw the calf and the people dancing, his anger waxed hot. He cast the tables out of his hands and broke them beneath the mount. He then took the calf which they had made and burned it in the fire, ground it to powder, threw it upon the water and made the people of Israel drink of it.

Poor little Aaron, trying to pacify his brother Moses, endeavored to put the blame upon the people, saying they had asked for gods. He even went so far as to say that he took their gold and cast it into the fire and there came out a golden calf.

There is more to this wicked story. Aaron the priest had made them naked unto their shame among their enemies. When Moses saw all of this, he cried out, "Who is on the Lord's side?" The sons of Levi gathered themselves unto him. He then ordered them to take their swords and slay every man his brother, every man his companion, every man his neighbor. The children of Levi did according to the word of Moses, and there fell of the people that day about three thousand men.

4. *The confession of Moses.* He came before the Lord and poured out his heart. He didn't try to hide the sins of the people, but openly confessed, "Oh, this people have sinned a great sin, and have made them gods of gold."

Now notice the prayer of Moses as he prayed to be blotted out of God's book: "Yet now, if thou wilt forgive their sin—; and if not, blot me, I pray thee, out of thy book which thou hast written."

Let us take a few moments to note this prayer.

I. THE PRAYER OF A LONELY HEART

Yes, God was with him, but Moses was lonely because his people had fallen, because they turned away from God and had worshiped a golden calf. They had sinned in their every action, and Moses could not hide their sins. The great leader of Israel was almost by himself. Any man who stands for God will often find himself entirely alone.

It was lonely for Elijah on Mount Carmel. He stood alone. He prayed alone. It was lonely for Jeremiah when he was cast into the pit. His tears flowed copiously. He was alone save for the presence of God. It was lonely for Daniel when he was cast into the lions' den. It seemed that all had turned against him and away from him. It was lonely for the Apostle Paul when he was stoned and cast out of the city and left for dead.

I repeat: it will often be lonely for any child of God who has convictions and stands for them. It will be lonely for young people who determine to live for Jesus Christ. It will be lonely for a businessman who resolves to conduct his business by standards of righteousness. It will be lonely for the politician who strives to guide his public acts by divine commands. It will often be lonely for men and women who courageously stand for God.

Then, again, it was not lonely, for God was with Moses. This is His promise: "I will never leave thee, nor forsake thee." Moses felt the presence of God. He knew how to reach the throne of God. He could hear the voice of the Almighty.

In trouble, practice the upward look. Circumstances may be dark and devastating, but the upward look gives peace and courage. Remember—God never fails!

Lonely heart, look to Him. He will give you aid. Do not think that prayer is hard. Remember that you can pray anywhere and all the time, for there is no time, place or posture in and by which we cannot reverently feel the presence of God. Talent is not needed. Eloquence is out of place. Dignity is no recommendation. Come to God, knowing that He never fails when we pray in faith, believing.

Someone has said:

> However early in the morning you seek the gate of access, you find it already open; and however deep the midnight moment when you find yourself in the sudden arms of death, the

winged prayer can bring an instant Saviour, and this wherever you are. It needs not that you ascend some special Pisgah or Moriah. It needs not that you should enter some awful shrine or pull off your shoes on some holy ground.

Could a memento be reared on every spot from which an acceptable prayer has passed away, and on which a prompt answer has come down, we should find, "The Lord hath been here" inscribed on many a cottage hearth and many a dungeon floor. We should find it not only in Jerusalem's proud Temple and David's cedar galleries, but in the fisherman's cottage by the brink of the Gennesaret, and in the upper chamber where Pentecost began.

And, whether it be the field where Isaac went down to meditate or the rocky knoll where Israel wrestled or the den where Daniel gazed on the hungry lions and the lions gazed on him or the hillside where the Man of sorrows prayed all night—we should still discern the ladder's feet, let down from Heaven, the landing place of mercy, the starting place of prayer.

II. A PRAYER BORN OF LOVE

Did Moses love the people of Israel? Yes, with all his heart. He loved them with a holy love when he tore to pieces the golden calf and when he ordered the children of Levi to fall upon the men of Israel.

Prayer is best when it comes from a heart of love. Perhaps I should quickly say that prayer can only be offered when it comes out of a heart of love. Hate, fear and worry will clip the wings of prayer. We can only pray effectively when we pray in love.

Now look at Moses. He went to the Lord. Hear him as he said, "Ye have sinned a great sin: and now I will go up unto the Lord; perdventure I shall make an atonement for your sin." He confessed the sin of the people. "Oh, this people have sinned a great sin, and have made them gods of gold."

We see an evidence of the love of Moses for his people. He was willing to be blotted out that they might be saved. Or, if they should die, then he was willing to die with them.

Think today of your prayer life. Are you praying in love? Do you love others enough to pray for them? Are you praying for your

Christian friends? praying for the unsaved? Certainly love must be one of the primary requisites for successful prayer.

III. A PRAYER OF EXTREMITY

Moses, the leader of Israel, felt that he had failed. When he turned his back, these people fell into sin. We can almost feel the desperation in this great man's voice as he cries to the Lord. It seems he had come to the end of the way. Nothing more could he do.

Some people pray in the hour of desperation, yet they have no grounds for prayer.

I am reminded of the story of the man who was repairing the roof of a house. As he worked near the top of the building, his feet began to slip, and he started sliding down the long roof. He kept slashing at the roof with his hammer, trying to stop his fall. When he saw that he could not stop himself, he called upon God in a loud voice to save him. As he did so, suddenly his hammer caught in the roof, and his downward progress ceased.

As he came to a stop, he ceased praying and began to curse loudly and profanely.

Such a man did not pray at all. That was no answer to his prayer, because he was not praying with a clean heart.

But thanks be unto God, He does answer when we come to Him in our hour of extremity. Someone has said, "Our extremity is God's opportunity." When we have gone as far as we can, it is then that our Heavenly Father comes to give us aid.

Think of the wonders of prayer. Someone has penned:

> Abraham's servant prays, and Rebecca appears. Jacob wrestles and prays and prevails with God. Esau's mind is wonderfully turned from the revengeful purpose he had harbored for twenty years.
>
> Moses prays, and Amalek is discomfited. Joshua prays, and Achan is discovered. Hannah prays, and Samuel is born. David prays, and Ahithophel hangs himself. Asa prays, and a victory is gained. Jehoshaphat prays, and God turns away his foes. Isaiah and Hezekiah pray, and 185,000 Assyrians are dead in twelve hours.

Daniel prays, and the lions are muzzled. Daniel prays, and the seventy weeks are revealed. Nehemiah prays, and the king's heart is softened in a minute. Elijah prays, and rain descends apace. Elisha prays, and Jordan is divided. Elisha prays, and a child's soul comes back, for prayer reaches eternity. Christians pray, and Peter is delivered by an angel.

Come to God with all your needs. Come in every time of extremity. Come when you feel life meaningless. Lay all before Him and wait for His help.

A woman, a dope fiend, became tired of living. In her hotel room she decided to commit suicide. But someone out there was praying for her. The radio was going and soon the voice of a minister came over the air. She heard the Gospel and called the preacher for an interview. After talking with him, she was saved. Instead of going to a suicide's grave, she found happiness in a good Christian life.

This is the picture of God's power. This is what He has been doing down through the centuries and will continue to do. The answer is prayer, prayer offered in the hour of extremity.

IV. THE PRAYER OF A TRUSTING SOUL

Moses' faith in God is illustrated in every part of his life. From the burning bush to Mount Nebo he exhibited his faith. He believed God in Egypt, believed God at the Red Sea, believed God when manna came down from Heaven.

As I read the story in Exodus 32, especially in the last half dozen verses of the chapter, I see Moses coming as a child before the Heavenly Father. He comes to pray and to believe God.

When does a man begin to grow spiritually? He begins to grow when he begins to pray. In every building the first stone must be laid and the first blow struck. The ark was 120 years in building, yet there was a day when Noah laid his ax to the first tree he cut down to form it. The Temple of Solomon was a glorious building. There was a day when the first huge stone was laid at the foot of Mount Moriah.

When is the beginning of spiritual growth? When you begin to pray.

Moses believed God to do what was right. It was not a matter of seeing or understanding, but of simply trusting the Lord. Nothing gives more peace than simply praying and trusting God to do what is best for us. "And we know that all things work together for good to them that love God, to them who are the called according to his purpose" (Rom. 8:28).

Such a concept of prayer should be ours. Trust God, have faith in Him and know that He will do what is best.

From this magnificent story we learn that the trusting soul will pray for others. Prayer and selfishness do not abide together. To pray truly, we must be unselfish about our prayers. This means remembering others in prayer, bringing them to God and calling upon Him to work in their lives.

At the close of a prayer meeting, the pastor observed a little girl about twelve years of age remaining upon her knees when most of the congregation had retired. Thinking that the child had fallen sleep, he touched her and told her it was time to return home. To his surprise he found that she was praying. He said, "All things whatsoever ye shall ask in prayer, believing, ye shall receive."

She looked at her pastor earnestly and inquired, "Is it so? Does God say that?"

When he took up a Bible and read the passage aloud, she immediately commenced praying, "Lord, send my father to the church. Lord, send my father here to church." She continued for about half an hour. Her earnest cry attracted the attention of those who had lingered about the door.

At last a man rushed into the church, up the aisle, and sank upon his knees by the side of his child, exclaiming, "What do you want of me?" She threw her arms about his neck and began to pray, "O Lord, convert my father." Soon the man's heart was melted, and he asked God to save him.

Later they found that the child's father was three miles from the church when she commenced praying for him. While packing goods in a wagon, he felt an irresistible impulse to return home. Driving rapidly to his house, he left the goods in the wagon and hasted to the church, where he found his daughter praying in his behalf.

Yes, the trusting soul will be praying for others.

Sinner friend, we are praying for you. Will you here and now repent of your sin and come to Jesus Christ? He is ready to save you. Listen to this verse: "But as many as received him, to them gave he power to become the sons of God, even to them that believe on his name" (John 1:12).

"Lord, Teach Us to Pray"

A Compilation of New Testament
Scriptures on Prayer
By
LEE ROBERSON
Pastor Emeritus, Highland Park Baptist Church
Chancellor-Founder, Tennessee Temple University,
Chattanooga, Tennessee

FOREWORD

Often in a midweek service or in a special PRAYER meeting I have heard the leader say, "Now, let us quote some of the great PRAYER promises of the Word. Who will be first?" Somebody will quote, 'Ask and ye shall receive....' Another, "If ye shall ask any thing in my name, I will do it." From there on the quotations are few and far between. Because of my own guilty ignorance and curiosity, I began to search out the PRAYER promises and examples in the New Testament. This little booklet is the result. I'm sure that I do not have all of the passages on PRAYER from the New Testament, but you will find the major ones listed here. PRAYER comments at the foot of the pages were gathered from various sources. In some cases I have given verses preceding and following the definite verse on PRAYER so that the thought might be clearer.

—LEE ROBERSON

The Model **Prayer**

*A*ND when thou prayest, thou shalt not be as the hypocrites *are*: for they love to pray standing in the synagogues and in the corners of the streets, that they may be seen of men. Verily I say unto you, They have their reward.

But thou, when thou prayest, enter into thy closet, and when thou hast shut thy door, pray to thy Father, which is in secret; and thy Father, which seeth in secret, shall reward thee openly.

But when ye pray, use not vain repetitions, as the heathen *do*: for they think that they shall be heard for their much speaking.

Be not ye therefore like unto them; for your Father knoweth what things ye have need of before ye ask him.

After this manner therefore pray ye: Our Father which art in heaven, Hallowed be thy name.

Thy kingdom come, Thy will be done in earth, as *it is* in heaven.

Give us this day our daily bread.

And forgive us our debts, as we forgive our debtors.

And lead us not into temptation, but deliver us from evil: For thine is the kingdom, and the power, and the glory, for ever. Amen.

For if ye forgive men their trespasses, your heavenly Father will also forgive you.

But if ye forgive not men their trespasses, neither will your Father forgive your trespasses.

—Matt. 6:5-15.

✦ ✦ ✦

"Some talk so much about the philosophy of PRAYER *that there is no time for the practice of* PRAYER.*"*

Ask, Seek, Knock

*A*sk, and it shall be given you; seek, and ye shall find; knock, and it shall be opened unto you:

For every one that asketh receiveth; and he that seeketh findeth; and to him that knocketh it shall be opened.

Or what man is there of you, whom if his son ask bread, will he give him a stone?

Or if he ask a fish, will he give him a serpent?

If ye then, being evil, know how to give good gifts unto your children, how much more shall your Father which is in heaven give good things to them that ask him?

—Matt. 7:7-11.

✦ ✦ ✦

"PRAYER *is asking God for something."*

A Cry to Christ

*T*HEN Jesus went thence, and departed into the coasts of Tyre and Sidon.

And, behold, a woman of Canaan came out of the same coasts, and cried unto him, saying, Have mercy on me, O Lord, thou son of David! my daughter is grievously vexed with a devil.

But he answered her not a word. And his disciples came, and besought him, saying, Send her away; for she crieth after us.

But he answered and said, I am not sent but unto the lost sheep of the house of Israel.

Then came she, and worshipped him, saying, Lord, help me!

But he answered and said, It is not meet to take the children's bread, and to cast it to dogs.

And she said, Truth, Lord: yet the dogs eat of the crumbs which fall from their masters' table.

Then Jesus answered and said unto her, O woman, great is thy faith: be it unto thee even as thou wilt. And her daughter was made whole from that very hour.

Matt. 15:21-28.

✦ ✦ ✦

"The devil has to work hard for all he gets in the home of a praying mother."

Praying With Others

*A*GAIN I say unto you, That if two of you shall agree on earth as touching any thing that they shall ask, it shall be done for them of my Father which is in heaven.

For where two or three are gathered together in my name, there am I in the midst of them.

—Matt. 18:19-20.

✦ ✦ ✦

When believers are one in PRAYER, *mighty power falls.*

Hypocritical Prayer

*W*OE unto you, scribes and Pharisees, hypocrites! for ye devour widows' houses, and for a pretence make long prayer: therefore ye shall receive the greater damnation.

—Matt. 23:14.

✦ ✦ ✦

"To spend and be spent in what is called the Lord's work when the life is prayerless is one of the devil's pet delusions."

Christ Agonizing in Prayer

*T*HEN cometh Jesus with them unto a place called Gethsemane, and saith unto the disciples, Sit ye here, while I go and pray yonder.

And he took with him Peter and the two sons of Zebedee, and began to be sorrowful and very heavy.

Then saith he unto them, My soul is exceeding sorrowful, even unto death: tarry ye here, and watch with me.

And he went a little farther, and fell on his face, and prayed, saying, O my Father, if it be possible, let this cup pass from me! nevertheless, not as I will, but as thou wilt.

And he cometh unto the disciples, and findeth them asleep, and saith unto Peter, What! could ye not watch with me one hour?

Watch and pray, that ye enter not into temptation; the spirit indeed is willing, but the flesh is weak.

He went away again the second time, and prayed, saying, O my Father, if this cup may not pass away from me, except I drink it, thy will be done.

And he came and found them asleep again: for their eyes were heavy.

And he left them, and went away again, and prayed the third time, saying the same words.

Then cometh he to his disciples, and saith unto them, Sleep on now, and take your rest; behold, the hour is at hand, and the Son of man is betrayed into the hands of sinners.

Rise, let us be going: behold, he is at hand that doth betray me.

—Matt. 26: 36-46.

✦ ✦ ✦

"Soldiers of the Lord are doing real fighting when they are on their knees."

The Morning Watch

AND in the morning, rising up a great while before day, he went out, and departed into a solitary' place, and there prayed.

And Simon, and they that were with him, followed after him.

And when they had found him, they said unto him, All *men* seek for thee.

—Mark 1:35-37.

✦ ✦ ✦

Giving Thanks

HE saith unto them, How many loaves have ye? go and see.   And when they knew, they say, Five, and two fishes.

And he commanded them to make all sit down by companies upon the green grass.

And they sat down in ranks by hundreds, and by fifties.

And when he had taken the five loaves and the two fishes, he looked up to heaven and blessed, and brake the loaves and gave *them* to his disciples to set before them; and the two fishes divided he among them all.

And they did all eat, and were filled.

And they took up twelve baskets full of the fragments, and of the fishes.

And they that did eat of the loaves were about five thousand men.

—Mark 6:38-44.

✦ ✦ ✦

Begin with God in the morning or He will be last in your thoughts all day and it will be a day of defeat.

Moving Mountains

*A*ND they come to Jerusalem; and Jesus went into the temple, and began to cast out them that sold and bought in the temple, and overthrew the tables of the moneychangers, and the seats of them that sold doves;

And would not suffer that any man should carry any vessel through the temple.

And he taught, saying unto them, Is it not written, My house shall be called of all nations the house of prayer? but ye have made it a den of thieves.

And the scribes and chief priests heard it, and sought how they might destroy him: for they feared him, because all the people was astonished at his doctrine.

And when even was come, he went out of the city.

And in the morning, as they passed by, they saw the fig tree dried up from the roots.

And Peter, calling to remembrance, saith unto him, Master, behold, the fig tree which thou cursedst is withered away!

And Jesus, answering, saith unto them, Have faith in God.

For verily I say unto you, That whosoever shall say unto this mountain, Be thou removed, and be thou cast into the sea; and shall not doubt in his heart, but shall believe that those things which he saith shall come to pass; he shall have whatsoever he saith.

Therefore I say unto you, What things soever ye desire when ye pray, believe that ye receive them, and ye shall have them.

And when ye stand praying, forgive, if ye have ought against any; that your Father also which is in heaven may forgive you your trespasses.

But if ye do not forgive, neither will your Father which is in heaven forgive your trespasses.

—Mark 11:15-26.

✦ ✦ ✦

"Nothing lies beyond the reach of PRAYER *except that which lies outside the will of God."*

Solitary **Praying**

*A*ND it came to pass, when he was in a certain city, behold a man full of leprosy; who seeing Jesus, fell on his face, and besought him, saying, Lord, if thou wilt, thou. canst make me clean.

And he put forth his hand and touched him, saying, I will; be thou clean. And immediately the leprosy departed from him.

And he charged him to tell no man, but go and shew thyself to the · priest, and offer for thy cleansing, according as Moses commanded, for a testimony unto them.

But so much the more went there a fame abroad of him: and great multitudes came together, to hear, and to be healed by him of their infirmities.

And he withdrew himself into the wilderness, and prayed.

—Luke 5:12-16.

"All Night"

*A*ND it came to pass in those days, that he went out into a mountain to pray, and continued all night in prayer to God.

And when it was day, he called unto him his disciples: and of them he chose twelve, whom also he named apostles.

—Luke 6:12-13.

✦ ✦ ✦

God's acquaintance cannot be made by hurried calls. He never bestows His richest gifts on hasty comers.

Prayer and a Miracle

*T*HEN he took the five loaves and the two fishes; and looking up to heaven, he blessed them, and brake, and gave to the disciples to set before the multitude.

And they did eat, and were all filled: and there was taken up of fragments that remained to them, twelve baskets.

—Luke 9:16, 17.

✦ ✦ ✦

"Alone Praying"

*A*ND it came to pass, as he was alone praying, his disciples were with him: and he asked them, saying, Whom say the people that I am?

—Luke 9:18.

✦ ✦ ✦

"A Christian is to PRAY *literally about everything."*

"As He **Prayed**"

*B*UT I tell you of a truth, there be some standing here, which shall not taste of death, till they see the kingdom of God.

And it came to pass, about an eight days after these sayings, he took Peter and John and James, and went up into a mountain to pray.

And as he prayed, the fashion of his countenance was altered, and his raiment was white and glistering.

And, behold, there talked with him two men, which were Moses and Elias:

Who appeared in glory, and spake of his decease which he should accomplish at Jerusalem.

But Peter and they that were with him were heavy with sleep: and when they were awake, they saw his glory, and the two men that stood with him.

And it came to pass, as they departed from him, Peter said unto Jesus, Master, it is good for us to be here: and let us make three tabernacles; one for thee, and one for Moses, and one for Elias: not knowing what he said.

While he thus spake, there came a cloud, and overshadowed them: and they feared as they entered into the cloud.

And there came a voice out of the cloud, saying, This is my beloved Son: hear him.

And when the voice was past, Jesus was found alone. And they kept it close, and told no man in those days any of those things which they had seen.

—Luke 9:27-36.

✦ ✦ ✦

PRAYER *changes people, places, and purposes.*

Jesus Talked to the Father

*I*N that hour Jesus rejoiced in spirit, and said, I thank thee, O Father, Lord of heaven and earth, that thou hast hid these things from the wise and prudent, and hast revealed them unto babes: even so, Father, for so it seemed good in thy sight.

All things are delivered to me of my Father; and no man knoweth who the Son is, but the Father; and who the Father is, but the Son, and *he* to whom the Son will reveal *him*.

—Luke 10:21, 22.

The Garden Prayer

*A*ND he came out, and went, as he was wont, to the mount of Olives; and his disciples also followed him.

And when he was at the place, he said unto them, Pray that ye enter not into temptation.

And he was withdrawn from them about a stone's cast, and kneeled down, and prayed.

Saying, Father, if thou be willing, remove this cup from me: nevertheless, not my will, but thine, be done.

And there appeared an angel unto him from heaven, strengthening him.

And being in an agony, he prayed more earnestly: and his sweat was as it were great drops of blood falling down to the ground.

And when he rose up from prayer, and was come to his disciples, he found them sleeping for sorrow,

And said unto them, Why sleep ye? rise and pray, lest ye enter into temptation.

—Luke 22:39-46.

✦ ✦ ✦

Satan may build a hedge about one and hinder his movements, but he cannot roof him in. When the outlook is bad, the uplook is always good.

Persistency in **Prayer**

*A*ND it came to pass, that as he was praying in a certain place, when he ceased, one of his disciples said unto him, Lord, teach us to pray, as John also taught his disciples.

And he said unto them, When ye pray, say, Our Father which art in heaven, Hallowed be thy name. . Thy kingdom come. Thy will be done, as in heaven, so in earth.

Give us day by day our daily bread.

And forgive us our sins; for we also forgive every one that is indebted to us. And lead us not into temptation; but deliver us from evil.

And he said unto them, Which of you shall have a friend, and shall go unto him at midnight, and say unto him, Friend, lend me three loaves;

For a friend of mine in his journey is come to me, and I have nothing to set before him?

And he from within shall answer and say, Trouble me not: the door is now shut, and my children are with me in bed; I cannot rise and give thee.

I say unto you, Though he will not rise and give him because he is his friend, yet because of his importunity he will rise and give him as many as he needeth.

And I say unto you, Ask, and it shall be given you; seek, and ye shall find; knock, and it shall be opened unto you.

For every one that asketh receiveth; and he that seeketh findeth; and to him that knocketh it shall be opened.

If a son shall ask bread of any of you that is a father, will he give him a stone? or if he ask a fish, will he for a fish give him a serpent?

Or if he shall ask an egg, will he offer him a scorpion?

If ye then, being evil, know how to give good gifts unto your children; how much more shall your heavenly Father give the Holy Spirit to them that ask him?

—Luke 11:1-13.

✦ ✦ ✦

"If PRAYER *is asking, then the answer to* PRAYER *must be receiving.*"

Pray for Helpers

*A*FTER these things the Lord appointed other seventy also, and sent them two and two before his face into every city and place, whither he himself would come.

Therefore said he unto them, The harvest truly is great, but the labourers are few: pray ye therefore the Lord of the harvest, that he would send forth labourers into his harvest.

—Luke 10:1-2.

✦ ✦ ✦

Zeal without PRAYER *is wasted energy.*

The **Prayer** on Calvary

*A*ND when they were come to the place, which is called Calvary, there they crucified him, and the malefactors, one on the right hand, and the other on the left.

Then said Jesus, Father, forgive them; for they know not what they do. And they parted his raiment, and cast lots.

—Luke 23:33, 34.

✦ ✦ ✦

Unless we PRAY *in Jesus' name and on the ground of His atoning work, we* PRAY *in vain.*

A **Prayer** From Hell

*A*ND in hell he lift up his eyes, being in torments, and seeth Abraham afar off, and Lazarus in his bosom.

And he cried and said, Father Abraham, have mercy on me, and send Lazarus, that he may dip the tip of his finger in water, and cool my tongue; for I am tormented in this flame.

But Abraham said, Son, remember that thou in thy lifetime receivedst thy good things, and likewise Lazarus evil things: but now he is comforted, and thou art tormented.

And beside all this, between us and you there is a great gulf fixed: so that they which would pass from hence to you cannot; neither can they pass to us, that would come from thence.

Then he said, I pray thee therefore, father, that thou wouldest send him to my father's house:

For I have five brethren; that he may testify unto them, lest they also come into this place of torment.

Abraham saith unto him, They have Moses and the prophets; let them hear them.

And he said, Nay, father Abraham: but if one went unto them from the dead, they will repent.

And he said unto him, If they hear not Moses and the prophets, neither will they be persuaded, though one rose from the dead.

—Luke 16:23-31.

✦ ✦ ✦

PRAYING *will make one lay aside his sinning or else sinning will make him lay aside his* PRAYING. *The two cannot work together.*

Prayer: Constant Calling on God

AND he spake a parable unto them *to this end*, that men ought always to pray, and not to faint;

Saying, There was in a city a judge, which feared not God, neither regarded man:

And there was a widow in that city; and she came unto him, saying, Avenge me of mine adversary.

And he would not for awhile: but afterward he said within himself, Though I fear not God, nor regard man;

Yet because this widow troubleth me, I will avenge her, lest by her continual coming she weary me.

And the Lord said, Hear what the unjust judge saith.

And shall not God avenge his own elect, which cry day and night unto him, though he bear long with them?

I tell you that he will avenge them speedily. Nevertheless, when the Son of man cometh, shall he find faith on the earth?

—Luke 18:1-8.

✦ ✦ ✦

He who fails to PRAY, *simply because the sun is shining and all is favorable, will find his power to* PRAY *gone when the storm clouds arise.*

Humility in **Prayer**

*A*ND he spake this parable unto certain which trusted in themselves that they were righteous, and despised others:

Two men went up into the temple to pray; the one a Pharisee, and the other a publican.

The Pharisee stood and prayed thus with himself: God, I thank thee that I am not as other men are, extortioners, unjust, adulterers, or even as this publican:

I fast twice in the week, I give tithes of all that I possess.

And the publican, standing afar off, would not lift up so much as his eyes unto heaven, but smote upon his breast, saying, God be merciful to me a sinner.

I tell you, this man went down to his house justified rather than the other: for every one that exalteth himself shall be abased; and he that humbleth himself shall be exalted.

—Luke 18:9-14.

✦ ✦ ✦

The PRAYER *that ascends the highest comes from the lowest depths of a humble and a contrite heart.*

God's House and **Prayer**

*A*ND he went into the temple, and began to cast out them that sold therein, and them that bought;

Saying unto them, It is written, My house is the house of prayer: but ye have made it a den of thieves.

And he taught daily in the temple. But the chief priests and the scribes and the chief of the people sought to destroy him,

And could not find what they might do: for all the people were very attentive to hear him.

—Luke 19:45-48.

Christ **Prays** for His Own

*A*ND the Lord said, Simon, Simon, behold, Satan hath desired to have you, that he may sift you as wheat:

But I have prayed for thee, that thy faith fail not: and when thou art converted, strengthen thy brethren.

And he said unto him, Lord, I am ready to go with thee, both into prison, and to death.

And he said, I tell thee, Peter, the cock shall not crow this day, before that thou shalt thrice deny that thou knowest me.

—Luke 22:31-34.

✦ ✦ ✦

"PRAYER *is a letter sent from earth to heaven.*"

A **Prayer** and a Promise

*A*ND he said unto Jesus, Lord, remember me when thou comest into thy kingdom.

And Jesus said unto him, Verily I say unto thee, To day shalt thou be with me in paradise.

—Luke 23:42, 43.

For whosoever shall call upon the name of the Lord shall be saved.

—Rom. 10:13.

The Ascension Blessing

*A*ND, behold, I send the promise of my Father upon you: but tarry ye in the city of Jerusalem, until ye be endued with power from on high.

And he led them out as far as to Bethany, and he lifted up his hands, and blessed them.

And it came to pass, while he blessed them, he was parted from them, and carried up into heaven.

And they worshipped him, and returned to Jeru-salem with great joy:

And were continually in the temple, praising and blessing God.   Amen.

—Luke 24: 49-53.

✦ ✦ ✦

"A child of God can see more on his knees than a philosopher on his tiptoes."

Jesus Praying

*J*ESUS therefore, again groaning in himself, cometh to the grave. It was a cave, and a stone lay upon it.

Jesus said, Take ye away the stone. Martha, the sister of him that was dead, saith unto him, Lord, by this time he stink-eth: for he hath been dead four days.

Jesus saith unto her, Said I not unto thee, that, if thou wouldest believe, thou shouldest see the glory of God?

Then they took away the stone from the place where the dead was laid. And Jesus lifted up his eyes, and said, Father, I thank thee that thou hast heard me.

And I knew that thou hearest me always: but because of the people which stand by I said it, that they may believe that thou hast sent me.

And when he thus had spoken, he cried with a loud voice, Lazarus, come forth.

And he that was dead came forth, bound hand and foot with graveclothes: and his face was bound about with a napkin. Jesus saith unto them, Loose him, and let him go.

—John 11:38-44.

✦ ✦ ✦

"Our God is a God who hears and answers PRAYER!*"*

Jesus **Prayed**—God Answered

*N*ow is my soul troubled; and what shall I say? Father, save me from this hour: but for this cause come I unto this hour.

Father, glorify thy name. Then came there a voice from heaven, saying, I have both glorified it, and will glorify it again.

The people therefore that stood by, and heard it, said that it thundered: others said, An angel spake to him.

Jesus answered and said, This voice came not because of me, but for your sakes.

Nów is the judgment of this world: now shall the prince of this world be cast out.

And I, if I be lifted up from the earth, will draw all men unto me.

This he said, signifying what death he should die.

—John 12:27-33.

"PRAYER *is more discussed and less practiced than any other doctrine.*"

Blessed Promise

*A*ND whatsoever ye shall ask in my name, that will I do, that the Father may be glorified in the Son.

If ye shall ask anything in my name, I will do *it*.

If ye love me, keep my commandments.

—John 14:13-15.

Prayer: Abiding in Christ

*I*F ye abide in me, and my words abide in you, ye shall ask what ye will, and it shall be done unto you.

—John 15:7.

✦ ✦ ✦

"The quickest way to get on your feet is to get on your knees."

Prayer and Fruit Bearing

*Y*E have not chosen me, but I have chosen you, and ordained you, that ye should go and bring forth fruit, and that your fruit should remain: that whatsoever ye shall ask of the Father in my name, he may give it you.

—John 15:16.

In Jesus' Name

*A*ND in that day ye shall ask me nothing. Verily, verily, I say unto you, Whatsoever ye shall ask the Father in my name, he will give it you.

Hitherto have ye asked nothing in my name: ask, and ye shall receive, that your joy may be full.

These things have I spoken unto you in proverbs: but the time cometh, when I shall no more speak unto you in proverbs, but I shall shew you plainly of the Father.

At that day ye shall ask in my name: and I say not unto you, that I will pray the Father for you.

—John 16:23-26.

✦ ✦ ✦

"Our ability to stay with God in the PRAYER *closet, is the measure of our ability to stay with God when we are outside of it."*

The Lord's Prayer

Christ's Prayer of Consecration.

*T*HESE words spake Jesus, and lifted up his eyes to heaven, and said, Father, the hour is come; glorify thy Son, that thy Son also may glorify thee:

As thou hast given him power over all flesh, that he should give eternal life to as many as thou hast given him.

And this is life eternal, that they might know thee the only true God, and Jesus Christ, whom thou hast sent.

I have glorified thee on the earth: I have finished the work which thou gavest me to do.

And now, O Father, glorify thou me with thine own self, with the glory which I had with thee before the world was.

I have manifested thy name unto the men which thou gavest me out of the world: thine they were, and thou gavest them me; and they have kept thy word.

Now they have known that all things whatsoever thou hast given me are of thee.

For I have given unto them the words which thou gavest me; and they have received them, and have known surely that I came out from thee, and they have believed that thou didst send me.

I pray for them: I pray not for the world, but for them which thou hast given me; for they are thine.

And all mine are thine, and thine are mine; and I am glorified in them.

And now I am no more in the world, but these are in the world, and I come to thee. Holy Father, keep through thine own name those whom thou hast given me, that they may be one, as we are.

While I was with them in the world, I kept them in thy name: those that thou gavest me I have kept, and none of them is lost, but the son of perdition; that the scripture might be fulfilled.

(*Continued on next page*)

And now come I to thee; and these things I speak in the world, that they might have my joy fulfilled in themselves.

I have given them thy word; and the world hath hated them, because they are not of the world, even as I am not of the world.

I pray not that thou shouldest take them out of the world, but that thou shouldest keep them from the evil.

They are not of the world, even as I am not of the world.

Sanctify them through thy truth: thy word is truth.

As thou hast sent me into the world, even so have I also sent them into the world.

And for their sakes I sanctify myself, that they also might be sanctified through the truth.

Neither pray I for these alone, but for them also which shall believe on me through their word;

That they all may be one; as thou, Father, art in me, and I in thee, that they also may be one in us: that the world may believe that thou hast sent me.

And the glory which thou gavest me I have given them; that they may be one, even as we are one:

I in them and thou in me, that they may be made perfect in one; and that the world may know that thou hast sent me, and hast loved them, as thou hast loved me.

Father, I will that they also, whom thou hast given me, be with me where I am; that they may behold my glory, which thou hast given me: for thou lovedst me before the foundation of the world.

O righteous Father, the world hath not known thee: but I have known thee, and these have known that thou hast sent me.

And I have declared unto them thy name, and will declare it: that the love wherewith thou hast loved me may be in them, and I in them.

—John 17.

✦ ✦ ✦

"PRAYER *means warfare and every time we* PRAY *we possess more of the enemy's ground.*"

Pre-Pentecost **Prayer** Meeting

*7*HEN returned they unto Jerusalem from the mount called Olivet, which is from Jerusalem a sabbath day's journey.

And when they were come in, they went up into an upper room, where abode both Peter, and James, and John, and Andrew, Philip, and Thomas, Bartholomew, and Matthew, James *the son* of Alphaeus, and Simon Zelotes, and Judas *the brother* of James.

These all continued with one accord in prayer and supplication, with the women, and Mary the mother of Jesus, and with his brethren.

—Acts 1:12-14.

✦ ✦ ✦

Prayer and Divine Guidance

*A*ND they appointed two, Joseph called Barsabas, who was surnamed Justus, and Matthias.

And they prayed, and said, Thou, Lord, which knowest the hearts of all *men,* shew whether of these two thou hast chosen,

That he may take part of this ministry and apostleship, from which Judas by transgression fell, that he might go to his own place.

And they gave forth their lots; and the lot fell upon Matthias; and he was numbered with the eleven apostles.

—Acts 1:23-26.

✦ ✦ ✦

"The more you pray, the more the Holy Spirit will push you out into service."

Prayer and Praise in the Early Church

*A*ND they continued steadfastly in the apostles' doctrine and fellowship, and in breaking of bread, and in prayers.

And fear came upon every soul: and many wonders and signs were done by the apostles.

And all that believed were together, and had all things common;

And sold their possessions and goods, and parted them to all men, as every man had need.

And they, continuing daily with one accord in the temple, and breaking bread from house to house, did eat their meat with gladness and singleness of heart,

Praising God, and having favour with all the people. And the Lord added to the church daily such as should be saved.

—Acts 2:42-47.

✦ ✦ ✦

"Why PRAY? *Because* PRAYER *is God's appointed way for Christians to have fulness of Joy."*

The Power of **Prayer**

*A*ND when they had prayed, the place was shaken where they were assembled together; and they were all filled with the Holy Ghost, and they spake the word of God with bóldness.

And the multitude of them that believed were of one heart and of one soul: neither said any of them that ought of the things which he possessed was his own; but they had all things common.

And with great power gave the apostles witness of the resurrection of the Lord Jesus: and great grace was upon them all.

—Acts 4:31-33.

✦ ✦ ✦

"Strength in PRAYER *is better than length in* PRAYER.*"*

The Importance of **Prayer** to the Apostles

*A*ND in those days, when the number of the disciples was multiplied, there arose a murmuring of the Grecians against the Hebrews, because their widows were neglected in the daily ministration.

Then the twelve called the multitude of the disciples unto them, and said, It is not reason that we should leave the word of God. and serve tables.

Wherefore, brethren, look ye out among you seven men of honest report, full of the Holy Ghost and wisdom, whom we may appoint over this business.

But we will give ourselves continually to prayer, and to the ministry of the word.

And the saying pleased the whole multitude; and they chose Stephen, a man full of faith and of the Holy Ghost, and Philip, and Prochorus, and Nicanor, and Timon, and Parmanas, and Nicolas a proselyte of Antioch:

Whom they set before the apostles; and when they had prayed, they laid their hands on them.

—Acts 6:1-6.

✦ ✦ ✦

"To whip the devil, fall on your knees."

The First Martyr **Prayed**

*W*HEN they heard these things, they were cut to the heart, and they gnashed on him with their teeth.

But he, being full of the Holy Ghost, looked up stedfastly into heaven, and saw the glory of God, and Jesus standing on the right hand of God,

And said, Behold, I see the heavens opened, and the Son of man standing on the right hand of God.

Then they cried out with a loud voice, and stopped their ears, and ran upon him with one accord,

And cast him out of the city, and stoned him: and the witnesses laid down their clothes at a young man's feet, whose name was Saul.

And they stoned Stephen, calling upon God, and saying, Lord Jesus, receive my spirit.

And he kneeled down, and cried with a loud voice, Lord, lay not this sin to their charge. And when he had said this, he fell asleep.

—Acts 7:54-60.

✦ ✦ ✦

"PRAY *hardest when it is hardest to* PRAY."

Prayer and a Miracle

*N*OW there was at Joppa a certain disciple named Tabitha, which by interpretation is called Dorcas: this woman was full of good works and almsdeeds which she did.

And it came to pass in those days, that she was sick, and died: whom, when they had washed, they laid her in an upper chamber.

And forasmuch as Lydda was nigh to Joppa, and the disciples had heard that Peter was there, they sent unto him two men, desiring him that he would not delay to come to them.

Then Peter arose, and went with them. When he was come, they brought him into the upper chamber: and all the widows stood by him weeping, and shewing the coats and garments which Dorcas made, while she was with them.

But Peter put them all forth, and kneeled down, and prayed; and turning him to the body, said, Tabitha, arise. And she opened her eyes: and when she saw Peter, she sat up.

And he gave her his hand, and lifted her up, and when he had called the saints and widows, presented her alive.

And it was known throughout all Joppa; and many believed in the Lord.

And it came to pass, that he tarried many days in Joppa, with one Simon, a tanner.

—Acts 9:36-43.

✦ ✦ ✦

"PRAYER *is not conquering God's reluctance, but laying hold of His willingness.*"

A Man of **Prayer**

*T*HERE was a certain man in Caesarea, called Cornelius, a centurion of the band called the Italian band.

A devout *man*, and one that feared God with all his house, which gave much alms to the people, and prayed to God alway.

He saw in a vision evidently, about the ninth hour of the day, an angel of God coming in to him, and saying unto him, Cornelius.

And when he looked on him, he was afraid, and said, What is it, Lord? And he said unto him, Thy prayers and thine alms are come up for a memorial before God.

—Acts 10:1-4 (Read all of chapter).

✦ ✦ ✦

"God's promises are always broader than our PRAYERS."

Answered Prayer

*P*ETER therefore was kept in prison; but prayer was made without ceasing of the church unto God for him.

And when Herod would have brought him forth, the same night Peter was sleeping between two soldiers, bound with two chains; and the keepers before the door kept the prison.

And, behold, the angel of the Lord came upon him, and a light shined in the prison; and he smote Peter on the side, and raised him up, saying, Arise up quickly. And his chains fell off from his hands.

And the angel said unto him, Gird thyself, and bind on thy sandals: and so he did. And he saith unto him, Cast thy garment about thee, and follow me.

And he went out, and followed him; and wist not that it was true which was done by the angel; but thought he saw a vision.

When they were past the first and the second ward, they came unto the iron gate that leadeth unto the city, which opened to them of his own accord; and they went out, and passed on through one street; and forthwith the angel departed from him.

And when Peter was come to himself, he said, Now I know of a surety, that the Lord hath sent his angel, and hath delivered me out of the hand of Herod, and from all the expectation of the people of the Jews.

And when he had considered the thing, he came to the house of Mary the mother of John, whose surname was Mark; where many were gathered together, praying.

And as Peter knocked at the door of the gate, a damsel came to hearken, named Rhoda.

And when she knew Peter's voice, she opened not the gate for gladness, but ran in, and told how Peter stood before the gate.

(*Continued on next page*)

And they said unto her, Thou art mad. But she constantly affirmed that it was even so. Then said they, It is his angel.

But Peter continued knocking: and when they had opened the door, and saw him, they were astonished.

—Acts 12:5-16.

✦ ✦ ✦

"Satan trembles when he sees the weakest saint upon his knees."

Paul **Prayed**

BRETHREN, my heart's desire and prayer to God for Israel is, that they might be saved.

For I bear them record, that they have a zeal of God, but not according to knowledge.

—Rom. 10:1, 2.

Prayer and Salvation

FOR there is no difference between the Jew and the Greek: for the same Lord over all is rich unto all that call upon him.

For whosoever shall call upon the name of the Lord shall be saved.

—Rom. 10:12, 13.

✦ ✦ ✦

"The religion of some people consists principally in PRAYING *that the Lord will provide."*

Prayer at Midnight

AND at midnight Paul and Silas prayed, and sang praises unto God: and the prisoners heard them.

And suddenly there was a great earthquake, so that the foundations of the prison were shaken: and immediately all the doors were opened, and every one's bands were loosed.

And the keeper of the prison awaking out of his sleep, and seeing the prison doors open, he drew out his sword, and would have killed himself, supposing that the prisoners had been fled.

But Paul cried with a loud voice, saying, Do thyself no harm; for we are all here.

Then he called for a light, and sprang in, and came trembling, and fell down before Paul and Silas,

And brought them out, and said, Sirs, what must I do to be saved?

And they said, Believe on the Lord Jesus Christ, and thou shalt be saved, and thy house.

And they spake unto him the word of the Lord, and to all that were in his house.

And he took them the same hour of the night, and washed *their* stripes; and was baptized, he and all his, straightway.

And when he had brought them into his house, he set meat before them, and rejoiced, believing in God with all his house.

Acts 16:25-34.

✦ ✦ ✦

"Anchor yourself to the Throne of God, then shorten the rope."

Prayer: A Weapon

PRAYING always with all prayer and supplication in the Spirit, and watching thereunto with all perseverance and supplication for all saints;

And for me, that utterance may be given unto me, that I may open my mouth boldly, to make known the mystery of the gospel.

—Eph. 6:18, 19.

Prayer and the Peace of God

BE careful for nothing; but in every thing by prayer and supplication, with thanksgiving, let your requests be made known unto God.

And the peace of God, which passeth all understanding, shall keep your hearts and minds through Christ Jesus.

—Phil. 4:6, 7.

✦ ✦ ✦

"The only way to do much for God is to ask much of God."

Prayer for Others

*F*OR this cause, we also, since the day we heard *it*, do not cease to pray for you, and to desire that ye might be filled with the knowledge of his will in all wisdom and spiritual understanding;

That ye might walk worthy of the Lord unto all pleasing, being fruitful in every good work, and increasing in the knowledge of God;

Strengthened with all might, according to his glorious power, unto all patience and longsuffering with joyfulness;

Giving thanks unto the Father, which hath made us meet to be partakers of the inheritance of the saints in light:

Who hath delivered us from the power of darkness, and hath translated *us* into the kingdom of his dear Son;

In whom we have redemption through his blood, *even* the forgiveness of sins.

—Col. 1:9-14.

✦ ✦ ✦

"PRAYING *men are essential to Almighty God in all His plans and purposes.*"

Unceasing **Prayer**

*P*RAY without ceasing.

In every thing give thanks, for this is the will of God in Christ Jesus concerning you.

Quench not the Spirit.

Despise not prophesyings.

Prove all things; hold fast that which is good.

Abstain from all appearance of evil.

And the very God of peace sanctify you wholly; and I pray God your whole spirit and soul and body be preserved blameless unto the coming of our Lord Jesus Christ.

Faithful is he that calleth you, who also will do it.

Brethren, pray for us.

Greet all the brethren with an holy kiss.

I charge you by the Lord, that this epistle be read unto all the holy brethren.

The grace of our Lord Jesus Christ be with you. Amen.

—I Thess. 5:17-28.

✦ ✦ ✦

"Failure to PRAY *is failure along the whole line of life."*

"Pray for Us"

*F*INALLY, brethren, pray for us, that the word of the Lord may have free course, and be glorified, even as it is with you:

And that we may be delivered from unreasonable and wicked men: for all men have not faith.

But the Lord is faithful, who shall stablish you, and keep you from evil.

—II Thess. 3:1-3.

Pray for Officials

I EXHORT therefore, that, first of all, supplications, prayers, intercessions, and giving of thanks, be made for all men;

For kings, and for all that are in authority; that we may lead a quiet and peaceable life in all godliness and honesty.

For this is good and acceptable in the sight of God our Saviour;

Who will have all men to be saved, and to come unto the knowledge of the truth.

For there is one God, and one mediator between God and men, the man Christ Jesus;

Who gave himself a ransom for all, to be testified in due time.

Whereunto I am ordained a preacher, and an apostle, (I speak the truth in Christ, and lie not;) a teacher of the Gentiles in faith and verity.

I will therefore that men pray everywhere, lifting up holy hands, without wrath and doubting.

—I Tim. 2:1-8.

✦ ✦ ✦

"PRAYER *is intended for God's ear. It is not man, but God who hears and answers* PRAYER."

Christic Our High Priest

SEEING then that we have a great high priest, that is passed into the heavens, Jesus the Son of God, let us hold fast our profession.

For we have not an high priest which cannot be touched with the feeling of our infirmities; but was in all points tempted like as we are, yet without sin.

Let us therefore come boldly unto the throne of grace, that we may obtain mercy, and find grace to help in time of need.

—Heb. 4:14-16.

✦ ✦ ✦

BY so much was Jesus made a surety of a better testament.

And they truly were many priests, because they were not suffered to continue by reason of death:

But this man, because he continueth ever, hath an unchangeable priesthood.

Wherefore he is able also to save them to the uttermost that

come unto God by him, seeing he ever liveth to make intercession for them.

For such an high priest became us, who is holy, harmless,
undefiled, separate from sinners, and made higher than the
heavens;

Who needeth not daily, as those high priests, to offer up
sacrifice, first for his own sins, and then for the people's: for
this he did once, when he offered up himself.

For the law maketh men high priests which have infirmity;
but the word of the oath, which was since the law, maketh the
Son, who is consecrated forevermore.

—Heb. 7:22-28.

✦ ✦ ✦

*H*AVING therefore, brethren, boldness to enter into the holiest
by the blood of Jesus,

By a new and living way, which he hath consecrated for us,
through the vail, that is to say, his flesh;

And having an high priest over the house of God;

Let us draw near with a true heart in full assurance of faith,
having our hearts sprinkled from an evil conscience, and our
bodies washed with pure water.

—Heb. 10:19-22.

✦ ✦ ✦

Pray in Faith

*I*F any of you lack wisdom, let him ask of God, that giveth
to all men liberally, and unbraideth not; and it shall be given
him.

But let him ask in faith, nothing wavering. For he that

wavereth is like a wave of the sea, driven with the wind and tossed.

For let not that man think that he shall receive any thing of the Lord.

A double minded man is unstable in all his ways.

—James 1:5-8.

✦ ✦ ✦

Asking Amiss

*Y*E ask, and receive not, because ye ask amiss, that ye may consume it upon your lusts.

Ye adulterers and adulteresses, know ye not that the friendship of the world is enmity with God? whosoever therefore will be a friend of the world, is the enemy of God.

Do ye think that the scripture saith in vain, The spirit that dwelleth in us lusteth to envy?

But he giveth more grace. Wherefore he saith, God resisteth the proud, but giveth grace unto the humble.

Submit yourselves therefore to God. Resist the devil, and he will flee from you.

Draw nigh to God, and he will draw nigh to you. Cleanse your hands, ye sinners; and purify your hearts, ye double minded.

Be afflicted, and mourn, and weep; let your laughter be turned to mourning, and your joy to heaviness.

Humble yourselves in the sight of the Lord, and he shall lift you up.

—James 4:3-10.

✦ ✦ ✦

"PRAYER *is measured, not by time, but by intensity.*"

Prayer for the Sick

*I*s any among you afflicted? let him pray. It any merry? let him sing psalms:

Is any sick among you? let him call for the elders of the church; and let them pray over him, anointing him with oil in the name of the Lord:

And the prayer of faith shall save the sick, and the Lord shall raise him up; and if he have committed sins, they shall be forgiven him.

Confess your faults one to another, and pray'one for another, that ye may be healed. The effectual fervent prayer of a right-ous man availeth much.

Elias was a man subject to like passions as we are, and he prayed earnestly that it might not rain; and it rained not on the earth by the space of three years and six months.

And he prayed again, and the heaven gave rain, and the earth brought forth her fruit.

—James 5:13-18.

✦ ✦ ✦

Prayer is a golden river at whose brink some die of thirst,
      While others kneel and drink.

God Hears the Righteous

*F*INALLY, *be ye* all of one mind, having compassion one of another; love as brethren, *be* pitiful, *be* courteous:

Not rendering evil for evil, or railing for railing; but contrariwise blessing; knowing that ye are there-unto called, that ye should inherit a blessing.

For he that will love life, and see good days, let him refrain his tongue from evil, and his lips that they speak no guile:

Let him eschew evil, and do good; let him seek peace, and ensue it.

For the eyes of the Lord *are* over the righteous, and his ears *are open* unto their prayers: but the face of the Lord *is* against them that do evil.

I Peter 3:8-12.

The End of the Age and **Prayer**

*B*UT the end of all things is at hand: be ye therefore sober, and watch unto prayer.

—I Peter 4:7.

✦ ✦ ✦

"Persevering PRAYER *always wins: God yields to importunity and fidelity."*

Confident **Prayer**

B ELOVED, if our heart condemn us not, then have we confidence toward God.

And whatsoever we ask, we receive of him, because we keep
his commandments, and do these things that are pleasing in his
sight.

—I John 3:21-22.

Prayer According to His Will

A ND this is the confidence that we have in him, that, if we
ask any thing according to his will, he heareth us:

And if we know that he hear us, whatsoever we ask, we
know that we have the petitions that we desired of him.

—I John 5:14-15.

✦ ✦ ✦

Scotch preacher's PRAYER: *"O Lord, guide us aright, for we
are verra, verra determined."*

Constructive **Prayer**

B UT ye, beloved, building up yourselves on your most holy
faith, praying in the Holy Ghost,

Keep yourselves in the love of God, looking for the mercy of
our Lord Jesus Christ unto eternal life.

And of some have compassion, making a difference:

And others save with fear, pulling them out of the fire; hat-
ing even the garment spotted by the flesh.

Now unto him that is able to keep you from falling, and to
present you faultless before the presence of his glory with exceeding joy,

To the only wise God our Saviour, be glory and majesty,
dominion and power, both now and ever. Amen.

—Jude 20-25.

✦ ✦ ✦

"Victory in life's conflict is impossible without PRAYER.*"*

Prayer—Too Late!

*A*ND the heaven departed as a scroll when it is rolled together: and every mountain and island were moved out of their places.

And the kings of the earth, and the great men, and the rich men, and the chief captains, and the mighty men, and every bondman, and every freeman, hid themselves in the dens and in the rocks of the mountains;

And said to the mountains and rocks, Fall on us, and hide us from the face of him that sitteth on the throne, and from the wrath of the Lamb:

For the great day of his wrath is come; and who shall be able to stand?

—Rev. 6:14-17.

✦ ✦ ✦

"PRAYER *is the genius and mainspring of life. Persistent non-praying eventually will depress life below zero."*

The Last Promise and Last **Prayer** in the Bible

*H*E which testifieth these things saith, Surely I come quickly. Amen. Even so, come, Lord Jesus.

The grace of our Lord Jesus Christ *be* with you all.   Amen.

—Rev. 22:20, 21.

✦ ✦ ✦

"The man of PRAYER, *whether layman or preacher, is God's right-hand man."*

For a complete list of books available from
the Sword of the Lord, write to Sword of
the Lord Publishers, P. O. Box 1099, Murfreesboro, Tennessee 37133.